crocheted animal hats

crocheted
animal hats

15 PROJECTS TO KEEP YOU WARM AND TOASTY

First published 2014 by
Guild of Master Craftsman Publications Ltd
Castle Place, 166 High Street, Lewes,
East Sussex BN7 1XU

ISBN 978 1 86108 974 8

A catalogue record for this book is available
from the British Library.

Publisher Jonathan Bailey
Production Manager Jim Bulley
Managing Editor Gerrie Purcell
Senior Project Editor Wendy McAngus
Editor Cath Senker
Managing Art Editor Gilda Pacitti
Designer Chloë Alexander
Photographer: Chris Gloag

Set in Neo Sans and Geometric Slabserif 712
Colour origination by GMC Reprographics
Printed and bound in China

contents

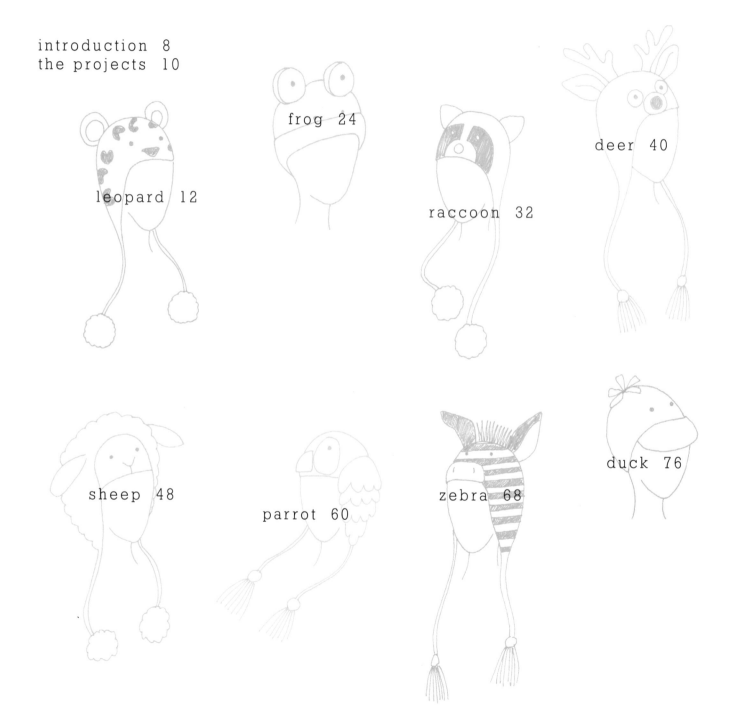

introduction

This book contains a collection of 15 crocheted animal-hat patterns in both children's and adults' sizes. The designs range from the monochrome striped zebra to the vibrantly coloured parrot, and from woodland creatures to safari animals.

At the back of the book (page 140) you will find instructions and tips on starting the projects as well as a guide to adding the finishing touches. There are two options for lining the hats to make them even cosier – you can choose between sewing a soft fleece fabric lining or crocheting a lining.

These animal hats are all crocheted in chunky yarn with the occasional feature – such as the rabbit's nose or the leopard's spots – worked in DK. This book will provide you with an array of cheerful headwear to make as a fun gift or to keep your own head warm and snuggly on a wintry day.

the projects

leopard

Keep warm in this wild-cat hat while making
a fashion statement at the same time with the
on-trend leopard print! This hat has generous
earflaps to keep out the winter chill.

MATERIALS

King Cole Merino Blend Chunky, 100% superwash
    wool (74yd/67m per 50g ball)
3[4] x 50g balls in 928 Old Gold (A)
King Cole Merino Blend DK, 100% superwash wool
    (123yd/112m per 50g ball)
1[1] x 50g ball in 048 Black (B)
King Cole Baby Alpaca DK, 100% pure baby alpaca
    (110yd/100m per 50g ball)
1[1] x 50g ball in 500 Camel (C)
3mm (UK11:US-), 5mm (UK6:USH/8) and 6mm
    (UK4:USJ/10) crochet hooks
2 x brown ¾[⅞]in (2[2.25]cm) diameter buttons
2 x black ½[⅝]in (1.25[1.5]cm) diameter buttons
Darning needle
Sewing needle
Black sewing thread
Small amount of toy stuffing
Thin card to make pompoms

SIZES

To fit: child, up to 20in (51cm) head circumference
[adult, up to 22in (56cm) head circumference]

TENSION

13 sts and 14 rows to 4in (10cm) over double
crochet on 6mm hook. Use larger or smaller hook
if necessary to obtain correct tension.

METHOD

The main part of the hat is crocheted in rounds, starting from the top and increasing the stitches to shape the crown. The earflaps are crocheted in rows and decreased to form the triangular shape. The leopard's ears are worked in rounds. They are lightly stuffed and attached to the hat along with a crocheted nose and leopard spots. The number of spots can be increased to create a denser pattern, if preferred. Buttons are stitched on for eyes.

MAIN PIECE
Both sizes

Starting at the top of the hat, with 6mm hook and A, make 4 ch and sl st to first ch to form a ring.

Round 1: 1 ch (does not count as a st), work 6 dc into ring, sl st into first dc (6 sts).

Round 2 (inc): 1 ch (does not count as a st), (dc2inc) 6 times, sl st into first dc (12 sts).

Round 3 (inc): 1 ch (does not count as a st), (dc2inc, 1 dc) 6 times, sl st into first dc (18 sts).

Round 4 (inc): 1 ch (does not count as a st), (dc2inc, 2 dc) 6 times, sl st into first dc (24 sts).

Round 5 (inc): 1 ch (does not count as a st), (dc2inc, 3 dc) 6 times, sl st into first dc (30 sts).

Round 6 (inc): 1 ch (does not count as a st), (dc2inc, 4 dc) 6 times, sl st into first dc (36 sts).

Round 7 (inc): 1 ch (does not count as a st), (dc2inc, 5 dc) 6 times, sl st into first dc (42 sts).

Round 8 (inc): 1 ch (does not count as a st), (dc2inc, 6 dc) 6 times, sl st into first dc (48 sts).

Round 9 (inc): 1 ch (does not count as a st), (dc2inc, 7 dc) 6 times, sl st into first dc (54 sts).

Round 10 (inc): 1 ch (does not count as a st), (dc2inc, 8 dc) 6 times, sl st into first dc (60 sts).

Main piece
Earflaps and edging
Child size

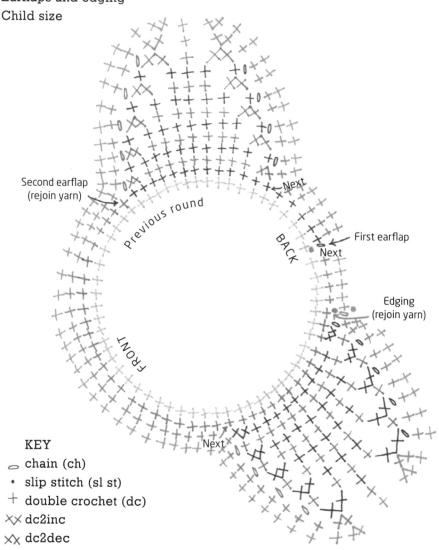

Second earflap (rejoin yarn)

Previous round

First earflap

Next

BACK

Next

Edging (rejoin yarn)

FRONT

Next

KEY
- ⌒ chain (ch)
- • slip stitch (sl st)
- + double crochet (dc)
- ✕✕ dc2inc
- ✕✕ dc2dec

Adult size only
Round 11 (inc): 1 ch (does not count as a st), (dc2inc, 9 dc) 6 times, sl st into first dc (66 sts).
Both sizes
Next: 1 ch (does not count as a st), work 1 dc in each dc, sl st into first dc. Rep last round 16 [18] times more.

Main piece
Follow rounds 11–13 of chart for adult size only

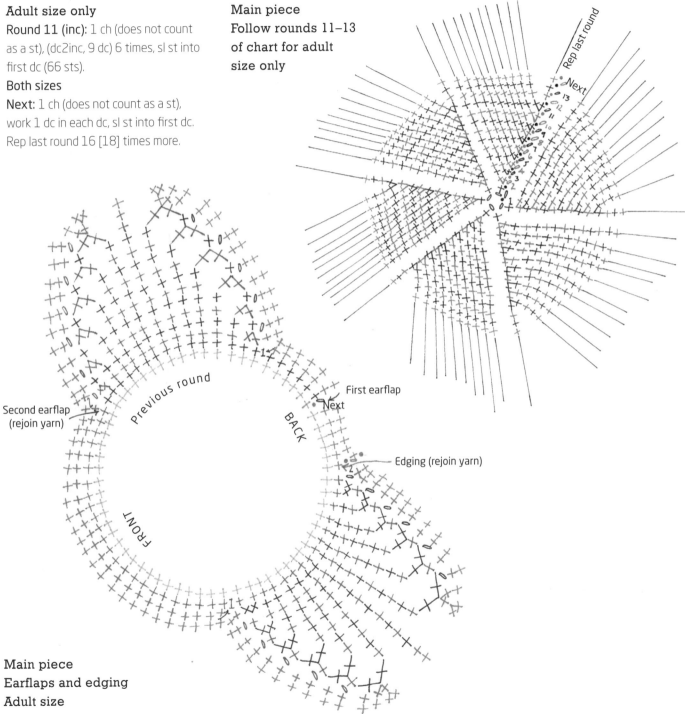

Rep last round

Next

Previous round

First earflap

Next

Second earflap (rejoin yarn)

BACK

Edging (rejoin yarn)

FRONT

Main piece
Earflaps and edging
Adult size

First earflap

Next: Starting at the centre back, 1 ch (does not count as a st), work 1 dc in next 5[6] dc.
The following is worked in rows:

Adult size only

Row 1 (RS): Work 1 dc in next 15 dc, turn.
Row 2 (WS) (dec): 1 ch (does not count as a st), dc2dec, 1 dc in next 11 dc, dc2dec, turn, 1 ch (does not count as a st).

Both sizes

Next: Work 1 dc in next 13 dc, turn.
Next (dec): *1 ch (does not count as a st), dc2dec, 1 dc in next 9 dc, dc2dec, turn (11 sts).
Next: 1 ch (does not count as a st), work 1 dc in each dc, turn.
Next (dec): 1 ch (does not count as a st), dc2dec, 1 dc in next 7 dc, dc2dec, turn (9 sts).
Next: 1 ch (does not count as a st), work 1 dc in each dc, turn.
Next (dec): 1 ch (does not count as a st), dc2dec, 1 dc in next 5 dc, dc2dec, turn (7 sts).
Next: 1 ch (does not count as a st), work 1 dc in each dc, turn.
Next (dec): 1 ch (does not count as a st), dc2dec, 1 dc in next 3 dc, dc2dec, turn (5 sts).
Next: 1 ch (does not count as a st), work 1 dc in each dc, turn.
Next (dec): 1 ch (does not count as a st), dc2dec, 1 dc in next 1 dc, dc2dec, turn (3 sts).*
Fasten off.

Second earflap

Next: With right side facing, rejoin A to the front of the hat. Work 1 dc in each of the 24 dc across the front of the hat.
The following is worked in rows:

Adult size only

Row 1 (RS): Work 1 dc in next 15 dc, turn.
Row 2 (WS) (dec): 1 ch (does not count as a st), dc2dec, 1 dc in next 11 dc, dc2dec, turn, 1 ch (does not count as a st).

Both sizes

Next: Work 1 dc in next 13 dc, turn.
Next: Work from * to * of first earflap.
Fasten off.

EARFLAP FACINGS (MAKE 2)

Omit if you plan to add a crocheted lining.

Both sizes

Using 6mm hook and A, make 14[16] ch.
Row 1 (RS): Work 1 dc in second ch from hook, 1 dc into the next 12[14] ch, turn (13[15] sts).

Adult size only

Row 2 (dec): 1 ch (does not count as a st), dc2dec, 1 dc in next 11 dc, dc2dec, turn (13 sts).
Row 3: 1 ch (does not count as a st), work 1 dc in each dc, turn.

Both sizes

Next: Work from * to * of the first earflap in the main piece pattern.
Fasten off.

Edging

Using 5mm hook and A, with right side of work facing and starting at row 1 of the earflap facing, work 1 dc into each stitch down the edge of the next 10[12] rows, work dc2inc, 1 dc, dc2inc in the next 3 dc along the lower edge of the earflap facing, work 1 dc into each stitch at the edge of the next 10[12] rows up the other side of the earflap facing (25[29] sts). Fasten off, leaving a long length of yarn at the end.

Child size

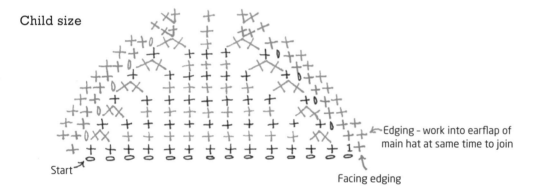

Start

Edging – work into earflap of main hat at same time to join

Facing edging

Adult size

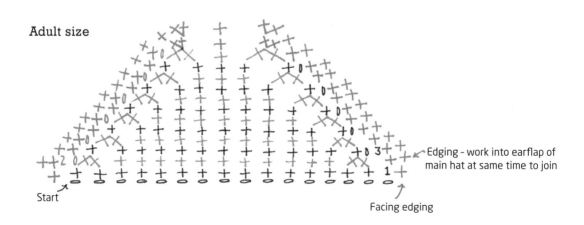

Start

Edging – work into earflap of main hat at same time to join

Facing edging

EARS (MAKE 2)

Both sizes

Starting at the top of the ear, with 6mm hook and A, make 4 ch and sl st to first ch to form a ring.

Round 1: 1 ch (does not count as a st), work 5 dc into ring, sl st into first dc (5 sts).

Round 2 (inc): 1 ch (does not count as a st), (dc2inc) 5 times, sl st into first dc (10 sts).

Round 3 (inc): 1 ch (does not count as a st), (dc2inc, 1 dc) 5 times, sl st into first dc (15 sts).

Round 4 (inc): 1 ch (does not count as a st), (dc2inc, 2 dc) 5 times, sl st into first dc (20 sts).

Adult size only

Next (inc): 1 ch (does not count as a st), (dc2inc, 4 dc) 4 times, sl st into first dc (24 sts).

Both sizes

Next: 1 ch (does not count as a st), work 1 dc in each dc, sl st into first dc.
Rep last round 4[6] more times.
Fasten off, leaving a long length of yarn at the end.

Child size

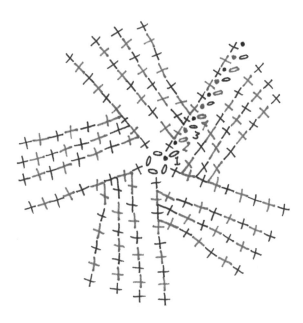

Adult size
Follow child's chart to end of round 4

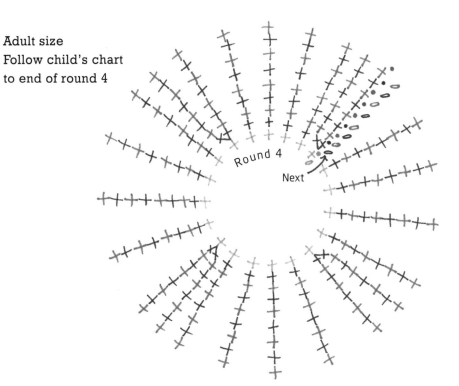

NOSE

Both sizes

With 3mm hook and B, make 4 ch and sl st to first ch to form a ring.

Next: 1 ch (does not count as a st), work 6 dc into ring, sl st into first dc (6 sts).

Child size only

Next round: 1 ch (does not count as a st), work 1 dc in each dc, sl st to first dc.

Next round (inc): 1 ch (does not count as a st), (dc2inc) 6 times, sl st into first dc (12 sts).

Next round (inc): 1 ch (does not count as a st), (dc2inc) 12 times, sl st into first dc (24 sts).

Adult size only

Next (inc): 1 ch (does not count as a st), (dc2inc) 6 times, sl st into first dc (12 sts).

Next round: 1 ch (does not count as a st), work 1 dc in each dc, sl st to first dc.

Next round: Rep last round.

Next round (inc): 1 ch (does not count as a st), (dc2inc) 12 times, sl st into first dc (24 sts).

Next round: 1 ch (does not count as a st), (dc2inc, 2 dc) 8 times, sl st into first dc (32 sts).

Both sizes

Fasten off, leaving a long length of yarn at the end.

Adult size

Child size

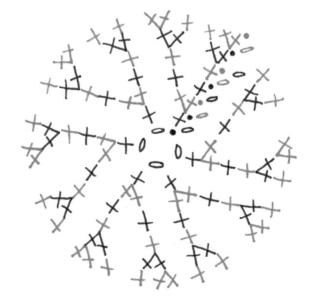

SPOTS

Tiny (make 10[10])

With 3mm hook and C, make 4 ch and sl st to first ch to form a ring.

Round 1: 1 ch (does not count as a st), work 5 dc into ring, sl st into first dc (5 sts).

Join in yarn B.

Round 2 (inc): With B, make 1 ch (does not count as a st), (dc2inc) 5 times (10 sts).

Fasten off, leaving a long length of B at the end.

Small (make 10[6])

With 3mm hook and C, make 4 ch and sl st to first ch to form a ring.

Row 1: 1 ch (does not count as a st), work 6 dc into ring, turn (6 sts).

Row 2 (inc): 1 ch (does not count as a st), (dc2inc) 3 times, join and continue in yarn B, (dc2inc) 3 times, turn (12 sts).

Row 3 (inc): With B, 1 ch (does not count as a st), (dc2inc, 1dc) 6 times (18 sts).

Fasten off, leaving a long length of B at the end.

Medium (make 6[6])

With 3mm hook and C, make 4 ch and sl st to first ch to form a ring.

Round 1: 1 ch (does not count as a st), work 5 dc into ring, sl st into first dc (5 sts).

Round 2 (inc): 1 ch (does not count as a st), (dc2inc) 5 times, sl st into first dc (10 sts).

Round 3 (inc): 1 ch (does not count as a st), (dc2inc, 1dc) twice, join and continue in yarn B, (dc2inc, 1dc) 3 times, sl st into first dc (15 sts).

Round 4 (inc): With B, 1 ch (does not count as a st), (dc2inc, 2dc) 4 times, sl st to next dc. Fasten off, leaving a long length of B at the end.

Large (make 0[6])

With 3mm hook and C, make 4 ch and sl st to first ch to form a ring.

Round 1: 1 ch (does not count as a st), work 6 dc into ring, sl st into first dc (6 sts).

Round 2 (inc): 1 ch (does not count as a st), (dc2inc) 6 times, sl st into first dc (12 sts).

Join in yarn B.

Round 3 (inc): With B, make 1 ch (does not count as a st), (dc2inc, 1dc) 6 times, turn (18 sts).

Next: With B, miss first dc, 1 dc in next 2 dc, (dc2inc, 2dc) 3 times, sl st to next dc. Fasten off, leaving a long length of B at the end.

Small

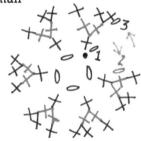

Large

Tiny

Medium

MAKING UP
Edging

With right side of work facing, using 5mm hook and A, rejoin yarn to the back of the hat by the second earflap.

Next: Work 1 dc in each of the 10[12] dc across the back of the hat, work 1 dc into each stitch down the edge of the next 9[11] rows of the first earflap, **working in the next 3 dc along the lower edge of the earflap, dc2inc, 1 dc, dc2inc, work 1 dc into each stitch at the edge of the next 9[11] rows up the other side of the earflap**, work 1 dc into each of the next 24 dc across the front of the hat, work 1 dc into each stitch down the edge of the next 9[11] rows of the second earflap, rep from ** to ** to finish the edging on the second earflap, sl st to first dc (80[90] sts).

If making a crocheted lining, fasten off and miss out the next round of edging.

Next: 1 ch (does not count as a st), work 1 dc in each of the 10[12] dc across the back of the hat, ***with wrong sides together, working into the stitches of the earflap and earflap facing at the same time to join, miss the first dc of the earflap facing and work 1 dc into each of the next 10[12] dc, dc2inc, 1 dc into next dc, dc2inc, 1 dc into each of the next 10[12] dc, miss the last dc of the earflap facing***, work 1 dc into each of the next 24 dc across the front of the hat, rep from *** to *** to finish the edging on the second earflap (84[94] sts). Sl st to next st and fasten off.

Using a darning or tapestry needle and the long length of A left after fastening off, slip stitch the top edge of the earflap facings to the inside of the main piece.

Ears

Stuff the ears lightly, keeping a flattened shape. With the long length of yarn left, sew the stitches from each side of the last round together to join, forming a straight edge. Bring each corner at the lower edge to the middle to shape the ear and stitch together. Sew in place to each side of the head, stitching all around the lower edges to prevent them from flopping over.

Nose

Flatten the nose and sew the 12[16] stitches from each side of the top edge together. With the stitched edge at the top, sew the nose to centre front of hat, around ⅝in (1.5cm) from the lower edge.

Eyes and spots

Place the small black buttons over the larger brown buttons and sew in place for the eyes. Position the spots over the front and back of the hat. They can be used with either side facing up so you can create a symmetrical leopard print pattern with them or scatter them randomly. Stitch them in place using the long length of yarn left at the end.

Finishing touches

If making a crocheted lining, attach the twisted cords to the hat after inserting the lining. Weave in all the yarn ends. Make two twisted cords (see page 154) using A, each measuring 8[12]in (20[30]cm) long, using 6[8] strands of yarn. Make two 2[2⅜]in (5[6]cm) pompoms (see page 155) in A and attach each to one end of the twisted cord, then stitch the other end of the cord to the tip of the earflap.

LINING

See pages 142–5 for how to make and attach a cosy fleece or crocheted lining.

frog

This beanie-style hat features a turned-back brim in a ribbed-effect pattern, and is topped by a huge pair of bulbous eyes. It's the perfect hat if you want to stand out from the crowd!

MATERIALS

Hayfield Baby Chunky, 70% acrylic, 30% nylon
   (170yd/155m per 100g ball)
2[2] x 100g balls in 405 Applebob (A)
1[1] x 100g ball in 400 White (B)
5.5mm (UK5:USI/9) crochet hook
2 x black ¾[⅞]in (2[2.25]cm) diameter buttons
   for the eyes
2 x black ½in (1.25cm) diameter buttons for
   the nostrils
Darning needle
Sewing needle
Black thread
Small amount of toy stuffing

SIZES

To fit: child, up to 20in (51cm) head circumference
[adult, up to 22in (56cm) head circumference]

TENSION

13 sts and 14 rows to 4in (10cm) over double
crochet on 5.5mm hook. Use larger or smaller hook
if necessary to obtain correct tension.

METHOD

This pattern starts with the brim, which is worked in rows of double crochet, inserting the hook into the back loop only of each stitch to produce the rib effect. The short edges are joined to form a ring, and the piece is turned on its side to finish the band of ribbing. The main part of the hat is in rounds of double crochet, with the first round of stitches worked evenly around the edge of the ribbing. The shaping of the crown is formed by decreasing the stitches. The eyes are in rounds of double crochet and are stitched to the top of the hat. The brim is turned up and buttons are sewn in place to finish the eyes and nostrils.

KEY

- ⚬ chain (ch)
- • slip stitch (sl st)
- + double crochet (dc)
- ✕✕ dc2inc
- ✕✕ dc2dec
- ⊤ double crochet into back loop only
- ⊤ slip stitch into back loop of double crochet and chain at the same time to join

RIB

Both sizes

Starting at the side of the rib, with 5.5mm hook and A, make 16[18] ch.

Row 1: Work 1 dc in second ch from hook, 1 dc into the next 14[16] ch, turn (15[17] sts).

Row 2: 1 ch (does not count as a st), work 1 dc into the back loop only of each dc, turn.

The last row forms the rib pattern. Rep row 2 until work measures 18[20]in (46[51]cm), turn.

Join short edges

Next: With the short edges together, make 1 ch, sl st into the back loop of the first dc and the reverse side of the first chain stitch at the same time to join. Continue working a sl st into both stitches at the same time to the end of the row to join the seam. This will create a ridge at the centre back of the hat, which will form part of the rib when the brim is turned up. Turn the work to continue.

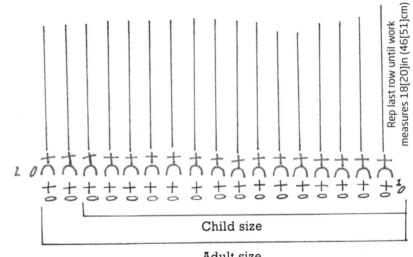

Rep last row until work measures 18[20]in (46[51]cm)

Child size

Adult size

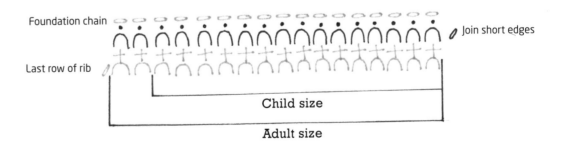

Foundation chain

Join short edges

Last row of rib

Child size

Adult size

The following is worked in rounds:

Crown

Round 1 (RS): 1 ch (does not count as
a st), work 60[66] dc evenly around the
edge of the ribbed brim, sl st to the first
dc (60[66] sts).

Round 2: 1 ch (does not count as
a st), work 1 dc in each dc, sl st to first dc.

Next: Rep the last round 9[12]
more times.

Crown
Child size

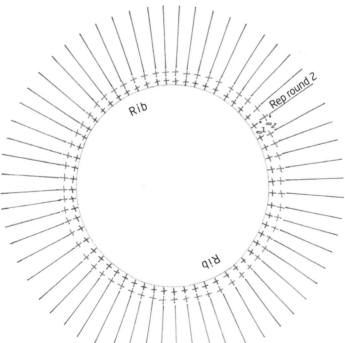

Crown
Adult size

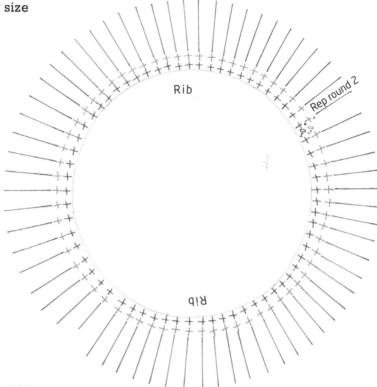

Shape crown
Adult size only
Next (dec): 1 ch (does not count as a st), (dc2dec, 9 dc) 6 times, sl st into first dc (60 sts).

Both sizes
Next (dec): 1 ch (does not count as a st), (dc2dec, 8 dc) 6 times, sl st into first dc (54 sts).

Next (dec): 1 ch (does not count as a st), (dc2dec, 7 dc) 6 times, sl st into first dc (48 sts).

Next (dec): 1 ch (does not count as a st), (dc2dec, 6 dc) 6 times, sl st into first dc (42 sts).

Shape crown
Child size – work from 2nd round of chart to end
Adult size – work from 1st round of chart to end

Next (dec): 1 ch (does not count as a st), (dc2dec, 5 dc) 6 times, sl st into first dc (36 sts).

Next (dec): 1 ch (does not count as a st), (dc2dec, 4 dc) 6 times, sl st into first dc (30 sts).

Next (dec): 1 ch (does not count as a st), (dc2dec, 3 dc) 6 times, sl st into first dc (24 sts).

Next (dec): 1 ch (does not count as a st), (dc2dec, 2 dc) 6 times, sl st into first dc (18 sts).

Next (dec): 1 ch (does not count as a st), (dc2dec, 1 dc) 6 times, sl st into first dc (12 sts).

Next (dec): 1 ch (does not count as a st), (dc2dec) 6 times, sl st into first dc (6 sts). Fasten off and weave in the end.

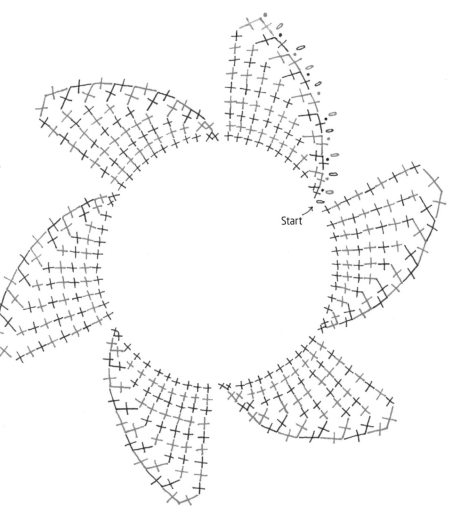

Start

EYEBALLS (MAKE 2)
Both sizes
Starting at the centre of the front of the eyeball, with 5.5mm hook and B, make 4 ch and sl st to first ch to form a ring.

*Round 1: 1 ch (does not count as a st), work 5 dc into ring, sl st into first dc (5 sts).

Round 2 (inc): 1 ch (does not count as a st), (dc2inc) 5 times, sl st into first dc (10 sts).

Round 3 (inc): 1 ch (does not count as a st), (dc2inc, 1 dc) 5 times, sl st into first dc (15 sts).

Round 4 (inc): 1 ch (does not count as a st), (dc2inc, 2 dc) 5 times, sl st into first dc (20 sts).

Adult size only
Next (inc): 1 ch (does not count as a st), (dc2inc, 3 dc) 5 times, sl st into first dc (25 sts).

Both sizes
Next: 1 ch (does not count as a st), work 1 dc in each dc, sl st to first dc. Rep last round twice more.*

Adult size only
Next (dec): 1 ch (does not count as a st), (dc2dec, 3 dc) 5 times, sl st into first dc (20 sts).

Eyeballs
Adult size – follow chart to end
Child size – follow chart to end of round 4

Both sizes
Next (dec): 1 ch (does not count as a st), (dc2dec, 2 dc) 5 times, sl st into first dc (15 sts).

Next (dec): 1 ch (does not count as a st), (dc2dec, 1 dc) 5 times, sl st into first dc (10 sts).

Fasten off, leaving a long length of yarn at the end.

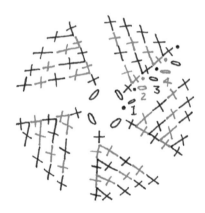

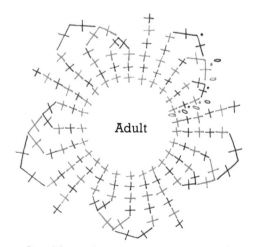

Round 6 to end

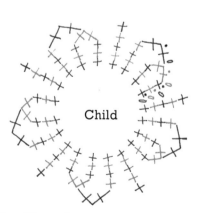
Round 5 to end

EYE SOCKETS (MAKE 2)
Both sizes

Starting at the centre of the back of the
eye socket, with 5.5mm hook and A, make
4 ch and sl st to first ch to form a ring.
Work from * to * of the eyeball.

Next: 1 ch (does not count as a st), work
1 dc into the back loop only of each dc,
sl st to first dc.

Fasten off, leaving a long length of yarn
at the end.

MAKING UP
Eyes

Stuff the eyeballs, weave the remaining
length of yarn through the last round
of stitches and draw up tight before
fastening off. Slip the eyeball inside the
eye socket and use the long length of
yarn left at the end of the socket to sew
it in place. Attach the eyes to the top
of the hat. Sew the large black buttons
to the centre of the eyeballs.

Finishing touches

Weave in all the ends. Sew the small
buttons in place on the front of the hat
for the nostrils.

LINING

See pages 142–5 for how to make and
attach a cosy fleece or crocheted lining.

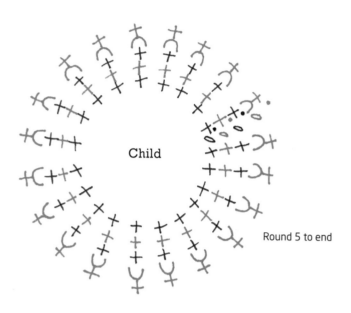

Child

Round 5 to end

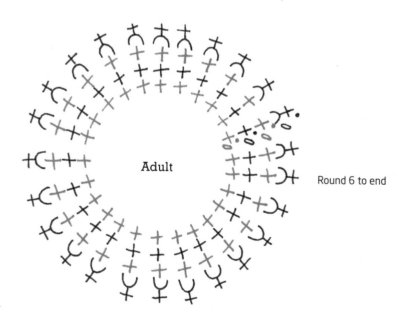

Adult

Round 6 to end

raccoon

Crocheted in dark grey yarn, the face and mask-like
features of the raccoon are worked in cream and black.
The striped cords have the characteristics
of the raccoon's ringed tail.

MATERIALS

Wendy Mode Chunky, 50% wool, 50% acrylic
    (153yd/140m per 100g ball)
2[2] x 100g balls in 244 Nightfall (A)
1[1] x 100g ball in 202 Vanilla (B)
1[1] x 100g ball in 220 Coal (C)
4.5mm (UK7:US7) and 5.5mm (UK5:USI/9) crochet
    hooks
2 x brown ¾[⅞]in (2[2.25]cm) diameter buttons
2 x black ½[⅝]in (1.25[1.5]cm) diameter buttons
Darning needle
Sewing needle
Black thread
Small amount of toy stuffing
Thin card to make pompoms

SIZES

To fit: child, up to 20in (51cm) head circumference
[adult, up to 22in (56cm) head circumference]

TENSION

13 sts and 14 rows to 4in (10cm) over double
crochet on 5.5mm hook. Use larger or smaller hook
if necessary to obtain correct tension.

METHOD

The main part of the hat is crocheted in one colour. The facial features are made in two curved sections worked in rows of double crochet that are shaped by increasing the stitches. The two pieces are joined using the main colour yarn and attached to the front of the hat. The ears are also made in two pieces and joined with a crocheted edging in a contrast colour. The button-shaped nose is worked in rounds. The twisted cords are made in two colours to produce the stripes, and the hat is finished with buttons for eyes and big pompoms.

MAIN PIECE

Both sizes

Starting at the top of the hat, with 5.5mm hook and A, follow the pattern for the leopard hat main piece on page 14.

EARFLAP FACINGS (MAKE 2)

Omit if you plan to add a crocheted lining.

Both sizes

With 5.5mm hook and A, follow the earflap facing pattern as for the leopard hat on page 18.

Edging

With 4.5mm hook and A, follow edging pattern for the earflap facing on page 18.

FACE

Both sizes

With 5.5mm hook and B, make 2 ch.

Row 1: Work 2[3] dc into second ch from hook, turn (2[3] sts).

Child size only

Row 2 (inc): 1 ch (does not count as a st), (dc2inc) twice, turn (4 sts).

Row 3 (inc): 1 ch (does not count as a st), (dc2inc, 1 dc) twice, turn (6 sts).

Row 4 (inc): 1 ch (does not count as a st), (dc2inc, 2 dc) twice, turn (8 sts). Join in C.

Row 5: With C, make 1 ch (does not count as a st), work 1 dc into each dc, turn.

Row 6 (inc): With C, make 1 ch (does not count as a st), (dc2inc, 3 dc) twice, turn (10 sts).

Row 7 (inc): With C, make 1 ch (does not count as a st), (dc2inc, 4 dc) twice, turn (12 sts).

Row 8 (inc): With C, make 1 ch (does not count as a st), (dc2inc, 5 dc) twice, turn (14 sts). Change to B.

Row 9 (inc): With B, make 1 ch (does not count as a st), (dc2inc, 6 dc) twice, turn (16 sts).

Row 10: With B, make 1 ch (does not count as a st), work 1 dc into each dc, turn.

KEY

⁀ chain (ch)
• slip stitch (sl st)
+ double crochet (dc)
✕✕ dc2inc

Face
Child size

Edging

Start face

← Join pieces

Work into each dc of both pieces at the same time to join

Face
Adult size

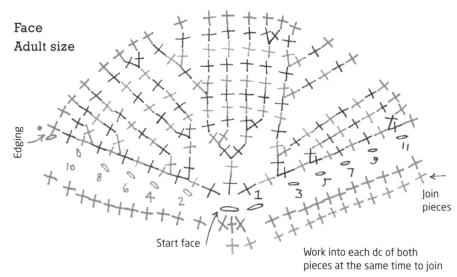

Edging

10 9 8 7 6 5 4 3 2 1

Start face

Work into each dc of both
pieces at the same time to join

Join pieces

Adult size only

Row 2: 1 ch (does not count as a st), work
1 dc into each dc, turn.

Row 3 (inc): 1 ch (does not count as a st),
(dc2inc) 3 times, turn (6 sts).

Row 4 (inc): 1 ch (does not count as a st),
(dc2inc, 1 dc) 3 times, turn (9 sts).
Join in C.

Row 5 (inc): With C, make 1 ch (does not
count as a st), (dc2inc, 2 dc) 3 times, turn
(12 sts).

Rows 6–7: With C, make 1 ch (does
not count as a st), work 1 dc into each
dc, turn.

Row 8 (inc): With C, make 1 ch (does not
count as a st), (dc2inc, 3 dc) 3 times, turn
(15 sts).

Row 9: With C, make 1 ch (does not count
as a st), work 1 dc into each dc, turn.
Change to B.

Row 10 (inc): With B, make 1 ch (does
not count as a st), (dc2inc, 4 dc) 3 times,
turn (18 sts).

Row 11 (inc): With B, make 1 ch (does
not count as a st), (dc2inc, 5 dc) 3 times,
turn (21 sts).

Both sizes
Edging

Join in A.

Next (RS): With A, make 1 ch (does not
count as a st), work 1 dc in each of the
16[21] dc, do not turn. Work 10[11]
dc evenly down the edge of the piece,
work 3 dc into the chain at the end, work
10[11] dc evenly up the edge of the
other side, sl st into the first dc
(39[46] sts).
Fasten off.
Make one more to match the first.

Join pieces

Place the right sides together, matching
the curved and straight edges. With
5.5mm hook, rejoin A and, starting at the

corner of the curve, work 1 dc into each
of the 12[13] dc down the straight edges
of both pieces at the same time to join.
Fasten off.

EARS (MAKE 2)
Both sizes

With 5.5mm hook and A, make 2 ch.

Row 1: Work 3 dc into second ch from
hook, turn (3 sts).

Row 2 (inc): 1 ch (does not count as a st),
dc2inc, 1 dc, dc2inc, turn (5 sts).

Row 3 (inc): 1 ch (does not count as
a st), dc2inc, 1 dc in next 3 dc, dc2inc,
turn (7 sts).

Row 4 (inc): 1 ch (does not count as
a st), dc2inc, 1 dc in next 5 dc, dc2inc,
turn (9 sts).

Row 5 (inc): 1 ch (does not count as
a st), dc2inc, 1 dc in next 7 dc, dc2inc,
turn (11 sts).

Row 6 (inc): 1 ch (does not count as
a st), dc2inc, 1 dc in next 9 dc, dc2inc,
turn (13 sts).

Adult size only

Next (inc): 1 ch (does not count as a st),
dc2inc, 1 dc in next 11 dc, dc2inc, turn
(15 sts).

Next (inc): 1 ch (does not count as a st),
dc2inc, 1 dc in next 13 dc, dc2inc, turn
(17 sts).

Both sizes

Next: 1 ch (does not count as a st), work
1 dc in each dc, turn.

Rep last row once more. Do not fasten off.

MAKING UP
Edging

With right side of work facing, using 4.5mm hook and A, rejoin yarn to the back of the hat by the second earflap.

Next: Work 1 dc in each of the 10[12] dc across the back of the hat, work 1 dc into each stitch down the edge of the next 9[11] rows of the first earflap, ** in the next 3 dc along the lower edge of the earflap work dc2inc, 1 dc, dc2inc; work 1 dc into each stitch at the edge of the next 9[11] rows up the other side of the earflap**. Do not fasten off.

Join face
Child size only
Work 1 dc in next dc.

Both sizes
With the wrong side of the face to the right side of the front of the hat and the lower edges aligned, work 1 dc in each of the next 22[24] dc of both the face edging and the front of the hat at the same time to join.

Child size only
Work 1 dc in next dc.

Both sizes
Work 1 dc into each stitch down the edge of the next 9[11] rows of the second earflap, rep from ** to ** to finish the edging on the second earflap, sl st to first dc (80[90] sts).
If making a crocheted lining, fasten off and miss out the next round of edging.

Next: 1 ch (does not count as a st), work 1 dc in each of the 10[12] dc across the back of the hat, ***with wrong sides together, working into the stitches of the earflap and earflap facing at the same time to join, miss the first dc of the earflap facing and work 1 dc into each of the next 10[12] dc, dc2inc, 1 dc into next dc, dc2inc, 1 dc into each of the next 10[12] dc, miss the last dc of the earflap facing***, work 1 dc into each of the next 24 dc across the front of the hat, rep from *** to *** to finish the edging to join the second earflap and earflap facing (84[94] sts).
Sl st to next st and fasten off.
Using a darning or tapestry needle and the long length of yarn left after fastening off, slip stitch the top edge of the earflap facings to the inside of the main piece.

Nose
Weave the length of yarn left after fastening off the nose through the last round of stitches. Pull the yarn to gather the opening and stitch securely. This will produce a flattened, round button-shaped nose. Sew the nose in place, just above the edging.

Ears
Push a thin layer of stuffing into the ears. With the length of yarn left after fastening off the edging, sew the lower edges of the inner and outer pieces together. Bring the two corners of each side from the lower edge of the ear to the middle to shape and stitch to hold in place, using the length of yarn B that was left after fastening off. Sew the ears to the main section of the hat, stitching all around the lower edges to keep them securely in place.

Finishing touches
If making a crocheted lining, attach the twisted cords to the hat after inserting the lining. Weave in all the yarn ends. Place the small black buttons over the larger brown buttons and sew in place for the eyes. Make two 8[12]in (20[30]cm)-long striped twisted cords (see page 154) using 3[4] strands each of yarn B and C. Make two 2[2⅜]in (5[6]cm) pompoms (see page 155) in A and attach each to one end of the twisted cord, then stitch the other end of the cord to the tip of the earflap.

LINING
See pages 142–5 for how to make and attach a cosy fleece or crocheted lining.

deer

Here is the perfect accessory to keep you warm on a breezy walk in the forest. Topped with a pair of antlers, this doe-eyed woodland creature is crocheted in a lightweight yarn.

MATERIALS

King Cole Magnum Lightweight Chunky 25% wool, 75% acrylic (120yd/110m per 100g ball)

2[2] x 100g balls in 366 Brown (A)

1[2] x 100g ball in 316 Pebble (B)

1[1] x 100g ball in 187 Charcoal (C)

4.5mm (UK7:US7) and 5.5mm (UK5:USI/9) crochet hooks

2 x dark brown ¾[⅞]in (2[2.25]cm) diameter buttons

2 x black ½[⅝]in (1.25[1.5]cm) diameter buttons

Darning needle

Sewing needle

Black thread

Small amount of toy stuffing

Thin card to make tassels

SIZES

To fit: child, up to 20in (51cm) head circumference [adult, up to 22in (56cm) head circumference]

TENSION

13 sts and 14 rows to 4in (10cm) over double crochet on 5.5mm hook. Use larger or smaller hook if necessary to obtain correct tension.

METHOD
The main piece is crocheted in rounds of double crochet with the earflaps worked in rows. The ears are made in two pieces each, crocheted in rows and stitched together before attaching to the hat. Unlike the ears in most of the other projects, they are not stuffed at all. The antlers, muzzle and nose are crocheted on a smaller hook to produce a tighter stitch and denser fabric. The antlers and muzzle are stuffed, and the hat is finished off with button eyes stitched over crocheted patches, and large tassels hanging from twisted cords.

MAIN PIECE
Both sizes
Starting at the top of the hat, with 5.5mm hook and A, follow the pattern for the leopard hat main piece on page 14.

Earflap facings (make 2)
Omit if you plan to add a crocheted lining.
Both sizes
With 5.5mm hook and B, follow the earflap facing pattern as for the leopard hat on page 18.
Edging
With 4.5mm hook and B, follow edging pattern for the earflap facing on page 18.

EARS (MAKE 2)
Both sizes
With 5.5mm hook and A, make 2 ch. Work rows 1–10 of the rabbit ears pattern on page 134.
Adult size only
Next: 1 ch (does not count as a st), work 1 dc in each dc, turn.
Next (inc): 1 ch (does not count as a st), dc2inc, 1 dc in next 11 dc, dc2inc, turn (15 sts).
Next: 1 ch (does not count as a st), work 1 dc in each dc, turn.
Next (inc): 1 ch (does not count as a st), dc2inc, 1 dc in next 13 dc, dc2inc, turn (17 sts).
Both sizes
Next: 1 ch (does not count as a st), work 1 dc in each dc, turn.
Rep last row 3 more times.
Fasten off, leaving a long length of yarn at the end.

INNER EARS (MAKE 2)

Both sizes

With 5.5mm hook and B, make 2 ch.
Work rows 1–10 of the rabbit inner ears pattern on page 136.

Adult size only

Next (inc): 1 ch (does not count as a st), dc2inc, 1 dc in next 7 dc, dc2inc, turn (11 sts).
Next: 1 ch (does not count as a st), work 1 dc in each dc, turn.
Rep last row once.
Next: 1 ch (does not count as a st), dc2inc, 1 dc in next 9 dc, dc2inc, turn (13 sts).

Both sizes

Next: 1 ch (does not count as a st), work 1 dc in each dc, turn.
Rep last row 3 more times.
Fasten off, leaving a long length of yarn at the end.

ANTLERS (MAKE 2)

Both sizes

With 4.5mm hook and B, make 15 ch and sl st to first ch to form a ring.
Round 1: 1 ch (does not count as a st), work 18 dc into ring, sl st into first dc (18 sts).
Round 2 (dec): 1 ch (does not count as a st), (dc2dec, 4 dc) 3 times, sl st into first dc (15 sts).
Round 3 (dec): 1 ch (does not count as a st), (dc2dec, 3 dc) 3 times, sl st into first dc (12 sts).
Round 4: 1 ch (does not count as a st), work 1 dc in each dc, sl st into first dc.
Next: Rep last round 2[4] more times.

Divide for first point

Next: 1 ch (does not count as a st), (dc2inc) 3 times, miss 6 dc, (dc2inc) 3 times, sl st into first dc.
Continue on these 12 sts.
Next: 1 ch (does not count as a st), work 1 dc in each dc, sl st into first dc.
Next: Rep last round 1[2] more times.

Divide for second point

Next: 1 ch (does not count as a st), dc2inc, work 1 dc in next 2 dc, miss next 6 dc, dc2inc, work 1 dc in next 2 dc, sl st into first dc.
Continue on these 8 sts.
Next: 1 ch (does not count as a st), work 1 dc in each dc, sl st into first dc.
Next: Rep last round 3[4] more times.

Shape top of antler

Next: 1 ch (does not count as a st), dc2dec, work 1 dc in next dc, (dc2inc) twice, work 1 dc in next dc, dc2dec, sl st into first dc.
Next: Rep last round 2 more times.
Next (dec): 1 ch (does not count as a st), dc2dec, work 1 dc in next 4 dc, dc2dec, sl st into first dc (6 sts).
Break yarn and weave through the last round of stitches, draw up to gather and fasten off.

Finish first and second points

Rejoin yarn to remaining round of 6 sts after dividing for the second point.
*Next: 1 ch (does not count as a st), work 1 dc in each dc, sl st into first dc.
Rep last round 3[4] more times. Break yarn and weave through the last round of stitches, draw up to gather and fasten off.*
Rejoin yarn to the 6 sts remaining for the first point. Rep from * to *.

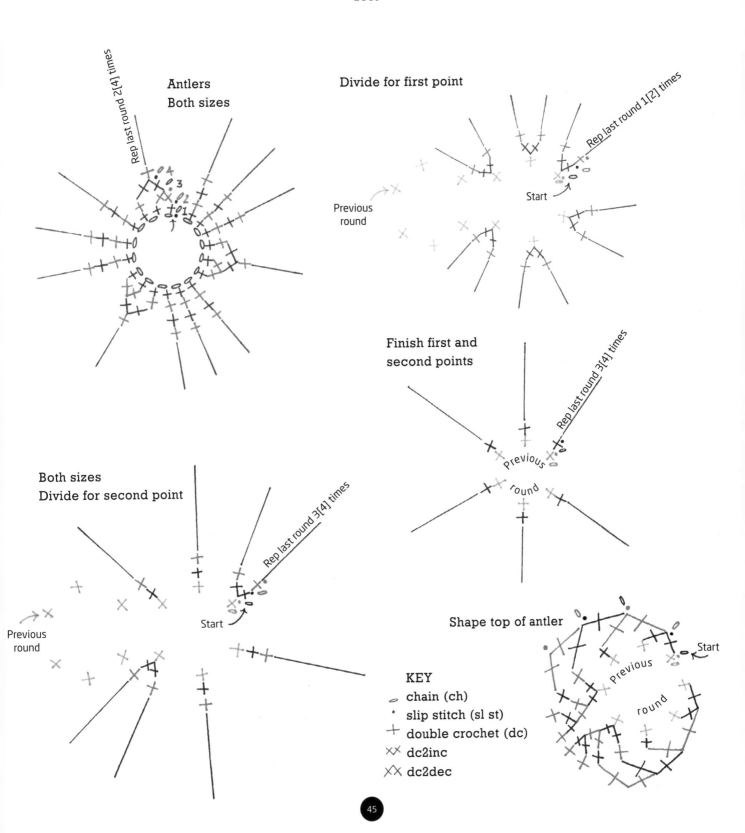

Antlers
Both sizes

Rep last round 2[4] times

Divide for first point

Rep last round 1[2] times

Start

Previous round

Finish first and
second points

Rep last round 3[4] times

Previous round

Both sizes
Divide for second point

Rep last round 3[4] times

Start

Previous round

Shape top of antler

Start

Previous round

KEY
- ⌢ chain (ch)
- • slip stitch (sl st)
- + double crochet (dc)
- ⚹ dc2inc
- ⚹ dc2dec

45

EYE PATCHES (MAKE 2)
Both sizes
Starting at the centre of the patch, with 4.5mm hook and B, make 4 ch and sl st to first ch to form a ring.

Round 1: 1 ch (does not count as a st), work 8 dc into ring, sl st into first dc (8 sts).

Round 2 (inc): 1 ch (does not count as a st), (dc2inc) 8 times, sl st into first dc (16 sts).

Fasten off, leaving a long length of yarn.

MUZZLE
Both sizes
With 4.5mm hook and B, make 4 ch and sl st to first ch to form a ring.

Round 1: 1 ch (does not count as a st), work 6 dc into ring, sl st into first dc (6 sts).

Round 2 (inc): 1 ch (does not count as a st), (dc2inc) 6 times, sl st into first dc (12 sts).

Round 3 (inc): 1 ch (does not count as a st), (dc2inc, 1 dc) 6 times, sl st into first dc (18 sts).

Child size only
Next: 1 ch (does not count as a st), work 1 dc in each dc, sl st into first dc.

Both sizes
Next (inc): 1 ch (does not count as a st), (dc2inc, 2 dc) 6 times, sl st into first dc (24 sts).

Next: 1 ch (does not count as a st), work 1 dc in each dc, sl st into first dc.

Adult size only
Next (inc): 1 ch (does not count as a st), (dc2inc, 3 dc) 6 times, sl st into first dc (30 sts).

Next: 1 ch (does not count as a st), work 1 dc in each dc, sl st into first dc.

Fasten off, leaving a long length of yarn at the end.

Eye patches

Muzzle
Child size

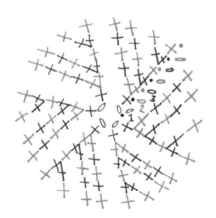

Nose
Child size

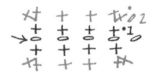

NOSE
Both sizes

With 4.5mm hook and C, make 5 ch.

Round 1: 1 dc into second ch from hook, 1 dc in next 2 ch, 2 dc in end ch, 1 dc down reverse side of ch, sl st into first dc (8 sts).

Round 2 (inc): 1 ch (does not count as a st), (dc2inc, 2 dc, dc2inc) twice, sl st into first dc (12 sts).

Adult size only

Round 3 (inc): 1 ch (does not count as a st), (dc2inc, 4 dc, dc2inc) twice, sl st into first dc (16 sts).

Fasten off, leaving a long length of yarn at the end.

MAKING UP
Edging

With right side of work facing, using 4.5mm hook and B, rejoin yarn to the back of the hat by the second earflap and follow the edging pattern as for the leopard hat on page 23.

Muzzle and nose

Use the long length of yarn left after fastening off to stitch the muzzle to the front of the hat, positioning it just above the edging, leaving a small opening. Push some stuffing into the opening to shape the muzzle before stitching it down. Sew the nose in place, horizontally, just above the centre of the muzzle.

Antlers and ears

With RS together sew the inner to the outer ear, leaving lower edge open. Turn RS out, positioning the inner ear so it sits centrally with a slight overlap each side of the larger outer piece. Join the lower edges. Bring the two corners of each side from the lower edge of the ear to the middle to shape. Stitch to hold in place. Attach to the main section of the hat, sewing all around the lower edge to keep them securely in place. Stuff the antlers firmly, using a pencil or knitting needle to push the stuffing right into the ends. Sew to the top of the hat, in between the ears, stitching all around the lower edges.

Finishing touches

If making a crocheted lining, attach the twisted cords to the hat after inserting the lining. Sew the patches to the hat, just above the muzzle with the wrong sides facing up. Place the small black buttons over the larger brown buttons and sew in place over the patches for the eyes. Weave in all the yarn ends. Make two twisted cords (see page 154) using A, each measuring 8[12]in (20[30]cm) long, using 6[8] strands of yarn. Make two tassels (see page 155) measuring 4[5⅛]in (10[13] cm) long in C, and attach each to one end of the twisted cord. Stitch the other end of the cord to the tip of the earflap.

LINING

See pages 142–5 for how to make and attach a cosy fleece or crocheted lining.

Muzzle
Adult size

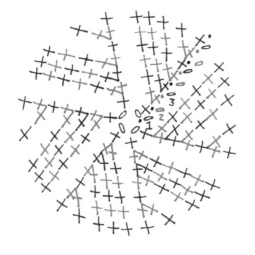

Nose
Adult size

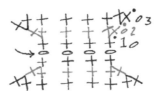

sheep

A bobble pattern forms the coat of this woolly chap.
Make a whole flock for all the family or swap the
black yarn for more of the cream to create
a different breed of sheep.

MATERIALS

King Cole Merino Blend Chunky, 100% superwash
    wool (74yd/67m per 50g ball)
4[4] x 50g balls in 919 Cream (A)
2[2] x 50g balls in 913 Black (B)
5mm (UK6:USH/8) and 6mm (UK4:USJ/10) crochet
    hooks
2 x white ¾[⅞]in (2[2.25]cm) diameter buttons
2 x black ½[⅝]in (1.25[1.5]cm) diameter buttons
Darning needle
Sewing needle
Black thread
Thin card to make pompoms

SIZES

To fit: child, up to 20in (51cm) head circumference
[adult, up to 22in (56cm) head circumference]

TENSION

13 sts and 14 rows to 4in (10cm) over double
crochet on 6mm hook.
13 sts and 11 rows to 4 in (10cm) over pattern on
6mm hook.
Use larger or smaller hook if necessary to obtain
correct tension.

SPECIAL ABBREVIATION

Make bobble (mb)

The bobble pattern appears on the reverse side of
the hat as you crochet. Yarn round hook, insert hook
into next st, catch yarn and draw back through stitch
(3 loops on hook), catch yarn again and draw through
2 loops (2 loops on hook), *yrh, insert hook into same
st, catch yarn and draw back through stitch (4 loops
on hook), catch yarn and draw through 2 loops*
(3 loops on hook), repeat from * to * 2 more times
(5 loops on hook), yrh, draw through all 5 loops.

METHOD

The hat is started from the top of the crown and worked in rounds. The pattern is formed on the reverse side of the hat, so the wrong side of the work will be facing you when the bobbles are crocheted. The shaping of the face is crocheted in rows with individual balls of yarn joined in to work each section of colour separately. The ears are worked in rounds of double crochet and are not stuffed, but are stitched into shape before attaching to the hat. Button eyes and an embroidered nose finish the look along with twisted cords and pompoms.

Main piece
Adult size

Child size
Follow chart to end of round 10

KEY

- ℴ chain (ch)
- • slip stitch (sl st)
- + double crochet (dc)
- ⅩⅩ dc2inc
- ⅩⅩ dc2dec
- bobble (mb)
- ☐ Yarn A
- ▨ Yarn B

MAIN PIECE

Both sizes

Starting at the top of the hat, with 6mm hook and A, make 4 ch and sl st to first ch to form a ring.

Round 1: 1 ch (does not count as a st), work 6 dc into ring, sl st into first dc (6 sts).

Round 2 (inc): 1 ch (does not count as a st), 1 dc in first dc, mb in the same dc, (1 dc in next dc, mb in the same dc) 5 times, sl st into first dc (12 sts/6 dc and 6 bobbles).

Round 3 (inc): 1 ch (does not count as a st), (dc2inc) 12 times, sl st into first dc (24 sts).

Round 4: 1 ch (does not count as a st), 1 dc in first dc, mb in next dc, (1 dc, mb) 11 times, sl st into first dc (12 dc and 12 bobbles).

Round 5 (inc): 1 ch (does not count as a st), (dc2inc, 1 dc) 12 times, sl st into first dc (36 sts).

Round 6: 1 ch (does not count as a st), 1 dc in first dc, mb in next dc, (1 dc, mb) 17 times, sl st into first dc (18 dc and 18 bobbles).

50

Round 7 (inc): 1 ch (does not count as a st), (dc2inc, 2 dc) 12 times, sl st into first dc (48 sts).

Round 8: 1 ch (does not count as a st), 1 dc in first dc, mb in next dc, (1 dc, mb) 23 times, sl st into first dc (24 dc and 24 bobbles).

Round 9 (inc): 1 ch (does not count as a st), (dc2inc, 3 dc) 12 times, sl st into first dc (60 sts).

Round 10: 1 ch (does not count as a st), 1 dc in first dc, mb in next dc, (1 dc, mb) 29 times, sl st into first dc (30 dc and 30 bobbles).

Adult size only

Next (inc): 1 ch (does not count as a st), (dc2inc, 9 dc) 6 times, sl st into first dc (66 sts).

Next: 1 ch (does not count as a st), 1 dc in first dc, mb in next dc, (1 dc, mb) 32 times, sl st into first dc (33 dc and 33 bobbles).

Shape face
Both sizes
Next: 1 ch (does not count as a st), work 1 dc in each dc, sl st into first dc.
The following is worked in rows:

Row 1: 1 ch (does not count as a st), 1 dc in first dc, mb in next dc, (1 dc, mb) 11[12] times, join in yarn B and work 1 dc in next 12[14] dc, join in a new ball of A here and work (mb, 1dc) 12[13] times, turn.

Row 2: With A, make 1 ch (does not count as a st), work 1 dc in next 23[25] dc, with B, work 1 dc in next 14[16] dc, with A, work 1 dc in next 23[25] dc, turn.

Row 3: With A, make 1 ch (does not count as a st), (1 dc, mb) 11[12] times, with B, work 1 dc in next 16[18] dc, with A, work (mb, 1dc) 11[12] times, turn.

Row 4: With A, make 1 ch (does not count as a st), work 1 dc in next 21[23] dc, with B, work 1 dc in next 18[20] dc, with A, work 1 dc in next 21[23] dc, turn.

Row 5: With A, make 1 ch (does not count as a st), (1 dc, mb) 10[11] times, with B, work 1 dc in next 20[22] dc, with A, work (mb, 1dc) 10[11] times, turn.

Row 6: With A, make 1 ch (does not count as a st), work 1 dc in next 19[21] dc, with B, work 1 dc in next 22[24] dc, with A, work 1 dc in next 19[21] dc, turn.

Row 7: With A, make 1 ch (does not count as a st), (1 dc, mb) 9[10] times, with B, work 1 dc in next 24[26] dc, with A, work (mb, 1dc) 9[10] times, turn.

Row 8: With A, make 1 ch (does not count as a st), work 1 dc in next 18[20] dc, with B, work 1 dc in next 24[26] dc, with A, work 1 dc in next 18[20] dc, turn.

Row 9: As row 7.
Row 10: As row 8.
Continue in yarn A.

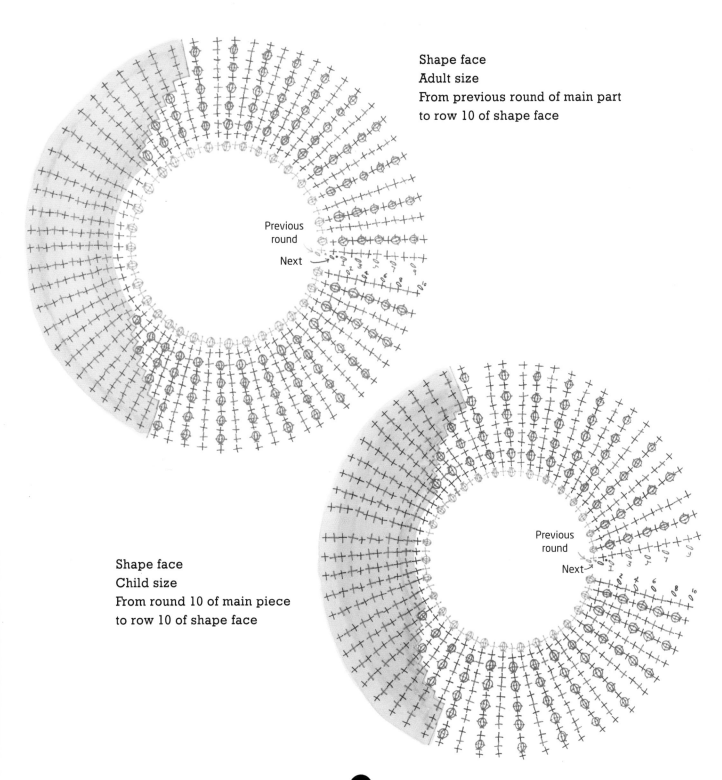

Shape face
Adult size
From previous round of main part
to row 10 of shape face

Previous
round

Next

Shape face
Child size
From round 10 of main piece
to row 10 of shape face

Previous
round

Next

First earflap

Next: 1 ch (does not count as a st), 1 dc in first 6[7] dc, (mb in next dc, 1 dc) 6[7] times, turn.

***Next (RS) (dec):** 1 ch (does not count as a st), (dc2dec) twice, 1 dc in next 5[7] dc, (dc2dec) twice, turn (9[11] sts).

Adult size only

Next: 1 ch (does not count as a st), 1 dc in first dc, (mb in next dc, 1 dc) 5 times, turn.

Next (dec): 1 ch (does not count as a st), dc2dec, 1 dc in next 7 dc, dc2dec, turn (9 sts).

Both sizes

Next: 1 ch (does not count as a st), 1 dc in first dc, (mb in next dc, 1 dc) 4 times, turn.

Next (dec): 1 ch (does not count as a st), dc2dec, 1 dc in next 5 dc, dc2dec, turn (7 sts).

Next: 1 ch (does not count as a st), 1 dc in first dc, (mb in next dc, 1 dc) 3 times, turn.

Next (dec): 1 ch (does not count as a st), dc2dec, 1 dc in next 3 dc, dc2dec, turn (5 sts).

Next (dec): 1 ch (does not count as a st), dc2dec, mb in next dc, dc2dec, turn (3 sts).

Next: 1 ch (does not count as a st), work 1 dc in each dc.*
Fasten off.

Second earflap

Next: With wrong side of hat facing and B, work 1 dc in each of the next 24 dc across the front of the hat, with A, work 1 dc in next dc, (mb in next dc, 1 dc) 6[7] times, turn.

Next: Work from * to * of first earflap.
Fasten off.

Earflaps
Adult size

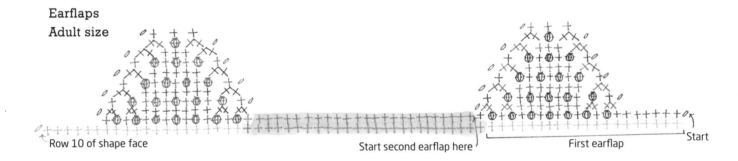

Row 10 of shape face

Start second earflap here

First earflap

Start

Earflaps
Child size

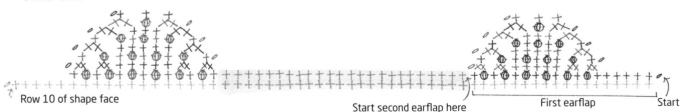

Row 10 of shape face

Start second earflap here

First earflap

Start

EARLFLAP FACINGS (MAKE 2)

Omit if you plan to add a crocheted lining.

Both sizes

With 6mm hook and A, follow the earflap facing pattern as for the leopard hat on page 18.

Edging

With 5mm hook and A, follow edging pattern for the earflap facing on page 18.

EARS (MAKE 2)

Both sizes

Starting at the top of the ear, with 6mm hook and B, make 4 ch and sl st to first ch to form a ring.

Follow the instructions and the chart as for the giraffe ears on page 116.

Fasten off, leaving a long length of yarn.

MAKING UP

Edging

Sew together the back seam of the hat. With right side of work facing, using 5mm hook and A, rejoin yarn to the back of the hat by the first earflap.

Next: Work 1 dc in each of the 10[12] dc across the back of the hat, work 9[11] dc evenly down the side of the second earflap, **working in the next 3 dc along the lower edge of the earflap, dc2inc, 1 dc, dc2inc; work 9[11] dc evenly up the other side of the earflap**, work 1 dc into each of the next 24 dc across the front of the hat, work 9[11] dc evenly down side of the first earflap, rep from ** to ** to finish the edging on the first earflap, sl st to first dc (80[90] sts).

If making a crocheted lining, fasten off and miss out the next round of edging.

Next: 1 ch (does not count as a st), work 1 dc in each of the 10[12] dc across the back of the hat, ***with wrong sides together, working into the stitches of the earflap and earflap facing at the same time to join, miss the first dc of the earflap facing and work 1 dc into each of the next 10[12] dc, dc2inc, 1 dc into next dc, dc2inc, 1 dc into each of the next 10[12] dc, miss the last dc of the earflap facing***, work 1 dc into each of the next 24 dc across the front of the hat, rep from *** to *** to finish the edging to join the remaining earflap and earflap facing (84[94] sts).

Sl st to next st and fasten off.

Using a darning or tapestry needle and the long length of yarn left after fastening off, slip stitch the top edge of the earflap facings to the inside of the main piece.

Ears

With the long length of yarn left, sew the stitches from each side of the last round of the ear together to join. Bring each corner of the ear to the middle to shape and stitch together. Work a running stitch around the lower edge and draw up the yarn to gather the stitches. Sew the ears in place to each side of the head, stitching all around the lower edges to attach them securely to the hat.

Finishing touches

If making a crocheted lining, attach the twisted cords to the hat after inserting the lining. Weave in all the yarn ends. Place the small black buttons over the larger white buttons and sew in place on the face for the eyes. Embroider the nose with a single fly stitch (see page 155) using yarn A. Make two twisted cords (see page 154) using B, each measuring 8[12] in (20[30]cm) long, using 6[8] strands of yarn. Make two 2[2⅜]in (5[6]cm) pompoms (see page 155) in A and attach each to one end of the twisted cord, then stitch the other end of the cord to the tip of the earflap. Weave the ends of yarn from the cords through the stitches of the earflap facings to prevent the black showing through the front of the earflaps.

LINING

See pages 142–5 for how to make and attach a cosy fleece or crocheted lining.

Making up
Edging
Adult size

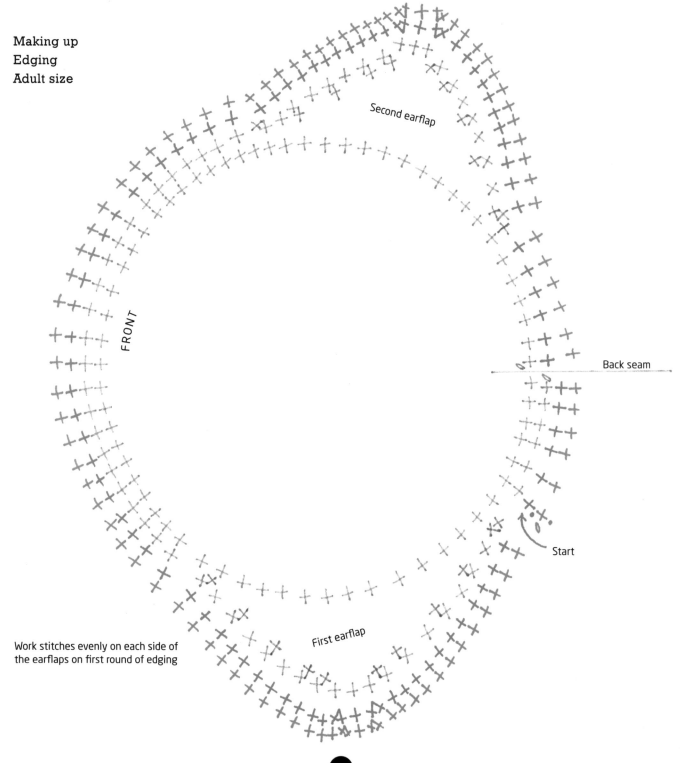

Second earflap

FRONT

Back seam

Start

First earflap

Work stitches evenly on each side of
the earflaps on first round of edging

Making up
Edging
Child size

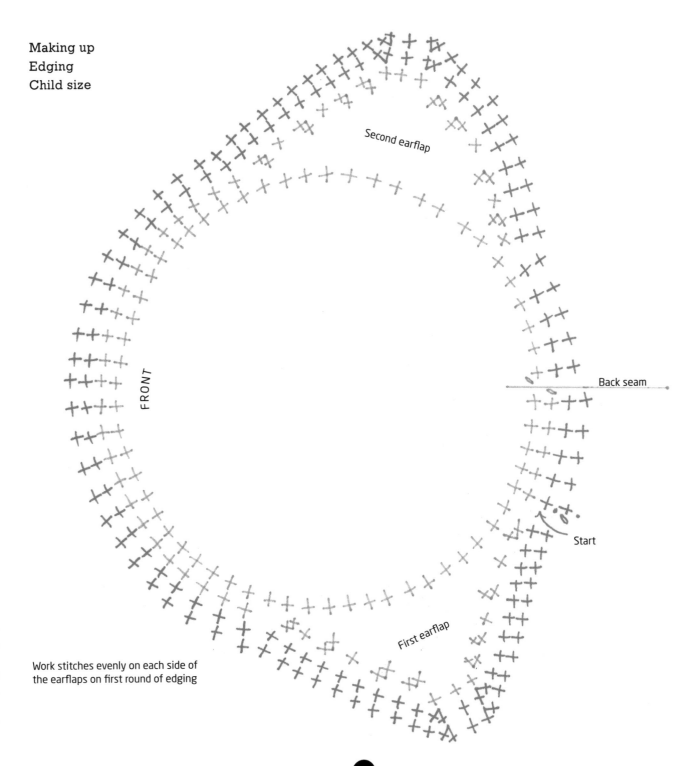

Second earflap

FRONT

Back seam

Start

First earflap

Work stitches evenly on each side of
the earflaps on first round of edging

parrot

Brighten up a dull day with a vibrant-coloured parrot hat and add some tropical fun to your winter wardrobe. This parrot even has feathery wings made with a special crochet stitch.

MATERIALS

King Cole Merino Blend Chunky, 100% superwash
    wool (74yd/67m per 50g ball)
3[3] x 50g balls in 921 Red (A)
2[2] x 50g balls in 859 Saxe (B)
1[1] x 50g ball in 928 Old Gold (C)
1[1] x 50g ball in 919 Cream (D)
Oddment of chunky yarn in black (E)
5mm (UK6:USH/8) and 6mm (UK4:USJ/10) crochet
    hooks
2 x black ⅝in (1.5cm) diameter buttons
Darning needle
Sewing needle
Black thread
Small amount of toy stuffing
Thin card to make tassels

SIZES

To fit: child, up to 20in (51cm) head circumference
[adult, up to 22in (56cm) head circumference]

TENSION

13 sts and 14 rows to 4in (10cm) over double
crochet on 6mm hook. Use larger or smaller hook
if necessary to obtain correct tension.

METHOD

The main piece is worked in rounds with the earflaps and facings in rows of double crochet. The spirals on the top of the hat, wings, eyes and beak use a smaller hook to produce a tighter stitch. The pattern that creates the feathery wings is crocodile stitch, which is formed by crocheting around the posts of the stitches on the previous row. The eyes are shaped by working in rounds of double crochet, half treble and treble stitches. The beak is a crocheted circle that is folded, stuffed and stitched to make a simple curved shape. The hat is finished off with small buttons, twisted cords and tassels.

MAIN PIECE
Both sizes

Starting at the top of the hat, with 6mm hook and A, follow the pattern for the leopard hat main piece on page 14.

EARFLAP FACINGS (MAKE 2)

Omit if you plan to add a crocheted lining.
Both sizes

With 6mm hook and B, follow the earflap facing pattern as for the leopard hat on page 18.
Edging

With 5mm hook and A, follow edging pattern for the earflap facing on page 18.

Spirals

With 5mm hook and B, join the yarn to a dc in the first round at the top of the hat.

Next: *Make 11[13] ch, 2 dc into second ch from hook, 2 dc into each of the next 9[11] ch, sl st into the same dc at the top of the hat; rep from * once more, sl st into next dc.

Next: Rep from * to make 2 spirals in each of the remaining 5 dc at the top of the hat (12 spirals).

Fasten off and weave in the ends.
Follow the chart for the spirals on the duck hat, page 79.

Wings (make 2)

Starting at the tip of the wing, with 5mm hook and B, make 9 ch.
Following the pattern for the owl wings on page 124, work rows 1–6 in B.
Work rows 7–12 in C.
Work rows 13 to end in A.
Fasten off, leaving a long length of yarn at the end.

EYES (MAKE 2)

With 5mm hook and D, make 4 ch and sl st to first ch to form a ring.

Round 1: 1 ch (does not count as a st), work 6[7] dc into ring, sl st to first dc (6[7] sts).

Round 2 (inc): 1 ch (does not count as a st), dc2inc into the first dc, htr2inc into the next dc, (tr2inc) 2[3] times, htr2inc, dc2inc, sl st to first dc (12[14] sts).

Round 3 (inc): 1 ch (does not count as a st), (dc2inc) 3[4] times, htr2inc into the next dc, (tr2inc) 4[4] times, htr2inc, (dc2inc) 3[4] times, sl st to first dc (24[28] sts).

Round 4 (inc): 1 ch (does not count as a st), 1 dc in next 8[9] sts, htr2inc, 1 tr into the next 2[3] sts, (tr2inc) 2[2] times, 1 tr in next 2[3] sts, htr2inc, 1 dc into the next 8[9] sts, sl st to first dc (28[32] sts). Join in yarn A.

Round 5 (inc): 1 ch (does not count as a st), work 1 dc in next 6[8] sts, (dc2inc, 2dc) 6[6] times, 1 dc in next 4[6] sts, sl st to first dc, turn (34[38] sts).

Fasten off, leaving a long length of yarn A at the end.

KEY
- ⌒ chain (ch)
- • slip stitch (sl st)
- + double crochet (dc)
- ⤬ dc2inc
- ⤬ dc2dec
- ⊤ htr2inc
- ⋁ treble (tr)
- ⏃ tr2inc

Eye
Child size

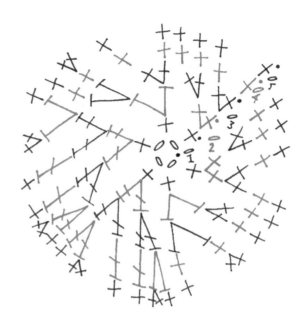

Eye
Adult size

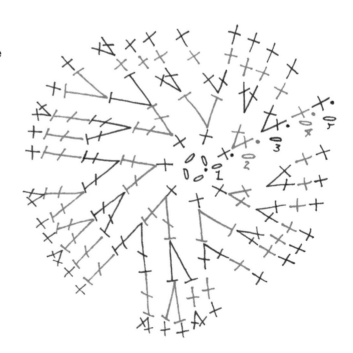

BEAK

With 5mm hook and E, make 4 ch and join with a sl st to first ch to form a ring.

Round 1: 1 ch (does not count as a st), work 6[7] dc into the ring (6[7] sts).

Round 2 (inc): 1 ch (does not count as a st), (dc2inc) 6[7] times, sl st to the first dc (12[14] sts).

Round 3 (inc): 1 ch (does not count as a st), (dc2inc, 1 dc) 6[7] times, sl st to the first dc (18[21] sts).

Round 4 (inc): 1 ch (does not count as a st), (dc2inc, 2 dc) 6[7] times, sl st to the first dc (24[28] sts).

Round 5 (inc): 1 ch (does not count as a st), (dc2inc, 3 dc) 6[7] times, sl st to the first dc (30[35] sts).

Round 6 (inc): 1 ch (does not count as a st), (dc2inc, 4 dc) 6[7] times, sl st to the first dc (36[42] sts).

Sl st to next st and fasten off leaving a long length of yarn.

Beak Child size

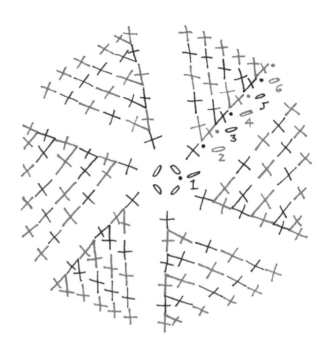

Beak Adult size

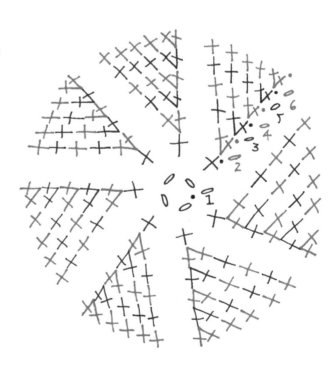

Key

- ⌒ chain (ch)
- • slip stitch (sl st)
- + double crochet (dc)
- ⋇ dc2inc

MAKING UP
Edging
With right side of work facing, using 5mm hook and A, rejoin yarn to the back of the hat by the second earflap and follow the edging pattern as for the leopard hat on page 23.

Eyes
Position the eyes on the front of the hat with the wider part just above the edging and sew all around the edges using the length of yarn left after fastening off. Work a few stitches into the centre to hold them in place with matching yarn. Sew a button to each, inside the first round of crochet, to finish the eyes.

Beak
Fold the crocheted circle in half. With the length of yarn left after fastening off, stitch the curved edges together, leaving a small opening. Push a little stuffing through the opening to fill the beak before stitching closed. Sew the beak in place in between the eyes with the curved side facing out, stitching all around it to secure it in position.

Wings
If making a crocheted lining, attach the wings and twisted cords to the ear flaps after inserting the lining. Press the wings with a cool iron. Position each wing over an earflap and sew in place, matching the colours of the yarn.

Finishing touches
Weave in all the yarn ends. Make two twisted cords (see page 154) using B, each measuring 8[12]in (20[30]cm) long, using 6[8] strands of yarn. Make two tassels (see page 155) measuring 4[5⅛] in (10[13]cm) long in B, and attach each to one end of the twisted cord, then stitch the other end of the cord to the tip of the earflap.

LINING
See pages 142–5 for how to make and attach a cosy fleece or crocheted lining.

zebra

This smart zebra hat in monochrome stripes with
its matching fringed mane and twisted cords is great
fun to wear. The detailed ears and nose with its
embroidered nostrils make it especially cute.

MATERIALS

James C Brett Chunky with Merino, 70% acrylic,
    20% siliconized soft polyamide, 10% merino
    wool (164yd/150m per 100g ball)
1[1] x 100g ball in CM1 (A)
2[2] x 100g balls in CM2 (B)
4.5mm (UK7:US7), 5mm (UK6:USH/8) and 6mm
    (UK4:USJ/10) crochet hooks
2 x white ¾[⅞]in (2[2.25]cm) diameter buttons
2 x black ½[⅝]in (1.25[1.5]cm) diameter buttons
Darning needle
Sewing needle
Black thread
Small amount of toy stuffing
Thin card to make tassels

SIZES

To fit: child, up to 20in (51cm) head circumference
[adult, up to 22in (56cm) head circumference]

TENSION

13 sts and 14 rows to 4in (10cm) over double
crochet on 6mm hook. Use larger or smaller hook
if necessary to obtain correct tension.

METHOD

The stripes are produced by alternating yarns every two rows. The black part of the ears is worked in rounds of double crochet with the white inners worked separately in rows and stitched on. The nose is crocheted using a smaller hook to create a firmer fabric and then stuffed to give it shape and finished with embroidered nostrils. A striped band worked in rows of double crochet with a fringe attached to one long edge forms the zebra's mane, which is stitched to the top and down the back of the hat.

MAIN PIECE

Both sizes

Starting at the top of the hat, with 6mm hook and A, make 4 ch and sl st to first ch to form a ring.

Round 1: 1 ch (does not count as a st), work 6 dc into ring, sl st into first dc (6 sts).

Round 2 (inc): 1 ch (does not count as a st), (dc2inc) 6 times, sl st into first dc (12 sts).

Join in yarn B.

Round 3 (inc): With B, make 1 ch (does not count as a st), (dc2inc, 1 dc) 6 times, sl st into first dc (18 sts).

Round 4 (inc): 1 ch (does not count as a st), (dc2inc, 2 dc) 6 times, sl st into first dc (24 sts).

Round 5 (inc): With A, make 1 ch (does not count as a st), (dc2inc, 3 dc) 6 times, sl st into first dc (30 sts).

Round 6 (inc): 1 ch (does not count as a st), (dc2inc, 4 dc) 6 times, sl st into first dc (36 sts).

Round 7 (inc): With B, make 1 ch (does not count as a st), (dc2inc, 5 dc) 6 times, sl st into first dc (42 sts).

Round 8 (inc): 1 ch (does not count as a st), (dc2inc, 6 dc) 6 times, sl st into first dc (48 sts).

Continue, following the pattern from round 9 of the leopard hat on page 14, alternating yarn A and B as before and finishing the last round of the child size in B and the last 2 rounds of the adult size in A.

First earflap

Both sizes

Next: With B, starting at the centre back, 1 ch (does not count as a st), work 1 dc in next 5[6] dc.

The following is worked in rows:

Row 1 (RS): With B, work 1 dc in next 13[15] dc, turn.

Adult size only

Next (WS) (dec): With B, make 1 ch (does not count as a st), dc2dec, 1 dc in next 11 dc, dc2dec, turn, 1 ch (does not count as a st).

Join in yarn A.

Next: With A, work 1 dc in next 13 dc, turn.

Both sizes

Next (dec): Continue as before, following the earflap pattern from * to * on page 16, and at the same time changing colour every two rows.

Work the last row of the earflap in child size in B.

Fasten off.

Second earflap

Next: With right side facing, rejoin B to the front of the hat. Work 1 dc in each of the 24 dc across the front of the hat. Complete the second earflap, following the pattern as for the leopard on page 16 and alternating the colours so the stripes match the first earflap.

EARFLAP FACINGS (MAKE 2)

Omit if you plan to add a crocheted lining.

Both sizes

With 6mm hook and A, follow the earflap facing pattern as for the leopard hat on page 18.

Edging

With 5mm hook and B, follow the edging pattern for the earflap facing on page 18.

EARS (MAKE 2)

Both sizes

Starting at the top of the ear, with 6mm hook and B, make 4 ch and sl st to first ch to form a ring.

Follow the instructions and the chart as for the giraffe ears on page 116.

Fasten off, leaving a long length of yarn.

INNER EARS (MAKE 2)

Both sizes

With 6mm hook and A, make 2 ch.

Row 1: Work 3 dc into second ch from hook, turn (3 sts).

Row 2: 1 ch (does not count as a st), work 1 dc in each dc, turn.

Row 3 (inc): 1 ch (does not count as a st), dc2inc, 1 dc, dc2inc, turn (5 sts).

Row 4: As row 2.

Row 5 (inc): 1 ch (does not count as a st), dc2inc, 1 dc in next 3 dc, dc2inc, turn (7 sts).

Row 6: As row 2.

Adult size only

Next (inc): 1 ch (does not count as a st), dc2inc, 1 dc in next 5 dc, dc2inc, turn (9 sts).

Both sizes

Next: As row 2.

Next: Rep last row 1[3] more times.

Fasten off, leaving a long length of yarn at the end.

KEY

⌒ chain (ch)

· slip stitch (sl st)

+ double crochet (dc)

XX dc2inc

Inner ear
Child size

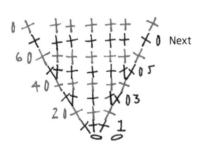

Inner ear
Adult size

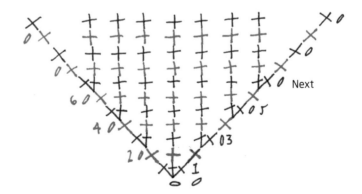

NOSE

Both sizes

With 4.5mm hook and B, make 4 ch and join with a sl st to the first ch to form a ring.

Round 1: 1 ch (does not count as a st), work 6 dc into ring, sl st to first dc (6 sts).

Round 2 (inc): 1 ch (does not count as a st), (dc2inc) 6 times, sl st into first dc (12 sts).

Round 3 (inc): 1 ch (does not count as a st), (dc2inc, 1 dc) 6 times, sl st into first dc (18 sts).

Round 4 (inc): 1 ch (does not count as a st), (dc2inc, 2 dc) 6 times, sl st into first dc (24 sts).

Round 5 (inc): 1 ch (does not count as a st), (dc2inc, 3 dc) 6 times, sl st into first dc (30 sts).

Adult size only

Next (inc): 1 ch (does not count as a st), (dc2inc, 4 dc) 6 times, sl st into first dc (36 sts).

Both sizes

Next round: 1 ch (does not count as a st), work 1 dc in each dc, sl st to first dc.
Rep last round 4[6] more times.
Fasten off, leaving a long length of yarn at the end.

Nose
Adult size
Child size – follow chart to end of round 5

Nose
Child size – round 5 to end

MANE

With 6mm hook and B, make 3 ch.

Row 1: Work 1 dc into second ch from hook, 1 dc in next ch, turn (2[2] sts).

Row 2: 1 ch (does not count as a st), work 1 dc in each dc, turn.

Join in A and rep row 2 twice.

Using yarn B, rep row 2 twice.

Continue in this way, working 2 rows of double crochet and at the same time alternating yarn A and B to create the stripes until you have completed 30[34] rows.

Fasten off.

Mane
Child and adult size

Rep until 30[34] rows completed

MAKING UP
Edging

With right side of work facing, using 5mm hook and B, rejoin yarn to the back of the hat by the second earflap and follow the edging pattern as for the leopard hat on page 23. Fasten off and slip stitch the top edge of the earflap facings to the inside of the main piece using yarn A.

Ears

Push a thin layer of stuffing into the ears, keeping the shape flat. With the long length of yarn left, sew the stitches from each side of the last round together to join, forming a straight edge. Sew the inner ear to the centre of the ear and aligning the lower edges. Bring each corner of the ear to the middle to shape and stitch together. Sew in place to each side of the head, stitching all around the lower edges to prevent them from flopping over.

Nose

Stuff the nose lightly to pad it out, keeping a flattened shape. Sew the stitches from each side of the last round together to form a straight edge. Stitch the nose in place on the front of the hat with the straight edge sitting just above the second row of edging stitches. Using yarn A and a blunt-ended darning needle, embroider the nostrils by working 2 straight stitches (see page 155) for each.

Eyes and mane

Place the small black buttons over the larger white buttons and sew in place for the eyes. To make the fringe of the mane, cut 14[16] sets of three 6in (15cm) lengths in yarn A and 16[18] sets of three lengths in B. Attach to the mane by folding three lengths in half to form a loop, inserting the crochet hook into the first stitch of the first stripe at the long edge and catching the looped yarn (**see 1**). Pull the loop a little way through,

remove the hook and then thread the ends back through the loop, pulling them tight (**see 2**). Repeat to the end of the mane, attaching one tassel to the edge of each row and matching the colours of the stripes. Trim the ends of the fringe and sew in place, starting at the lower edge of the back, matching the stripes up the centre back of the hat and ending at the second round at the front of the hat.

Finishing touches

If making a crocheted lining, attach the twisted cords to the hat after inserting the lining. Weave in all the yarn ends. Make two 8[12]in (20[30]cm)-long striped twisted cords (see page 154) using 3[4] strands each of yarn A and B. Make two tassels (see page 155) measuring 4[5⅛]in (10[13]cm) long in B, and attach each to one end of the twisted cord, then stitch the other end of the cord to the tip of the earflap.

LINING

See pages 142–5 for how to make and attach a cosy fleece or crocheted lining.

1

2

duck

This cheery yellow hat is sure to make you feel spring-like even in the depths of winter. The duck's bill forms a peak at the front of this beanie, while crocheted spirals produce a tuft of plumage to decorate the top.

MATERIALS

Katia Peru, 40% wool, 40% acrylic, 20% alpaca
    (116yd/106m per 100g ball)
2[2] x 100g balls in 021 (A)
1[1] x 100g ball in 022 (B)
5.5mm (UK5:USI/9) crochet hook
2 x white ¾[⅞]in (2[2.25]cm) diameter buttons
2 x black ½[⅝]in (1.25[1.5]cm) diameter buttons
Darning needle
Sewing needle
Black thread
Small amount of toy stuffing

SIZES

To fit: child, up to 20in (51cm) head circumference
[adult, up to 22in (56cm) head circumference]

TENSION

13 sts and 14 rows to 4in (10cm) over double
crochet on 5.5mm hook. Use larger or smaller hook
if necessary to obtain correct tension.

METHOD

This hat begins with the rib, which is worked in rows of double crochet through the back loops of the stitches. The short edges are joined by slip stitching the stitches together to form a ring, which is turned on its side to produce the ribbed effect. The first round of stitches of the crown is worked evenly around the stitches at the edge of the rib. The crown shaping is achieved by decreasing the stitches, and the main part of the hat is finished with spirals worked into the last round of stitches. These are made with a length of chain stitches. Two double crochet stitches are worked into each chain to make it twist. The duck's bill starts off with a foundation of chain stitches and then is crocheted in rounds, increasing the stitches to shape the piece. At the end, a round of decreasing is worked into the back loops of the stitches. The bill is stuffed and the opening stitched together. This forms a flat surface at the back. The bill is stitched to the hat through the front loops of the decrease row, creating a neat finish.

RIB

Both sizes

Starting at the side of the rib, with 5.5mm hook and A, make 6 ch.

Row 1: Work 1 dc in second ch from hook, 1 dc into the next 4 ch, turn (5[5] sts).

Row 2: 1 ch (does not count as a st), work 1 dc into the back loop only of each dc, turn.

The last row forms the rib pattern. Rep row 2 until work measures 18[20]in (46[51]cm).

KEY

- ∽ chain (ch)
- • slip stitch (sl st)
- + double crochet (dc)
- ✕✕ dc2inc
- ⋏⋏ dc2dec
- ⟊ double crochet into back loop only
- ⟟ slip stitch into back loop of double crochet and chain at the same time to join

Next: With the short edges together, make 1 ch, sl st into the back loop of the first dc and the reverse side of the first chain stitch at the same time to join. Continue working a sl st into both stitches at the same time to the end of the row to join the seam. This will create a ridge at the centre back of the hat, which will form part of the rib. Do not turn.

Rib
Adult and child size

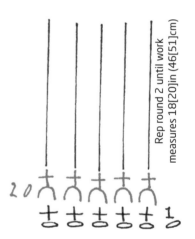

Rep round 2 until work measures 18[20]in (46[51]cm)

Foundation chain

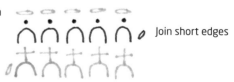

Join short edges

Last row of rib

The following is worked in rounds:
Follow the chart for the crown of the frog
hat on page 28.

Crown

Round 1 (RS): 1 ch (does not count as
a st), work 60[66] dc evenly around the
edge of the ribbed band, sl st to the first
dc (60[66] sts).

Round 2: 1 ch (does not count as a st),
work 1 dc in each dc, sl st to first dc.

Next: Rep the last round 11[14]
more times.

Shape crown

Work as for the crown shaping in the frog
pattern on page 29. Do not fasten off at
the end.

Spirals

*Make 11[13] ch, 2 dc into second ch
from hook, 2 dc into each of the next
9[11] ch, sl st into the same dc from the
last round of crown shaping; rep from *
once more, sl st into next dc.

Next: Rep from * to make 2 spirals in each
of the remaining 5 dc (12 spirals).
Fasten off, leaving a long length of yarn.
Weave the yarn through the 6 dc of the
last round of crown shaping and draw up
to gather and close the hole at the top
of the hat.

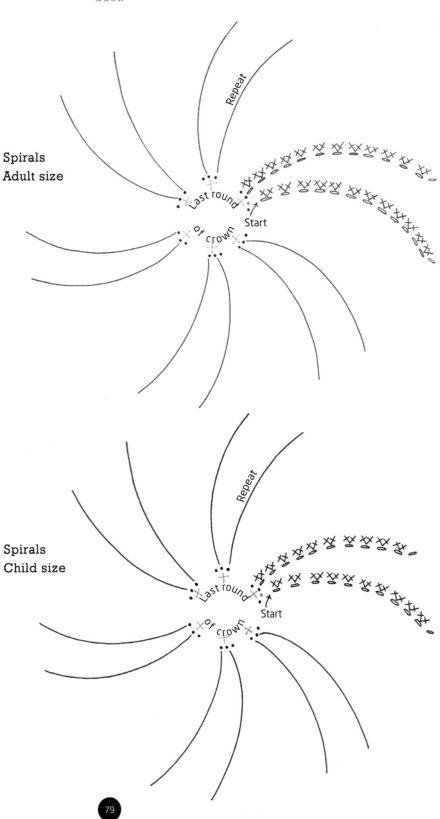

Spirals
Adult size

Spirals
Child size

BILL
Both sizes

With 5.5mm hook and B, make 9[11] ch.

Round 1 (RS): Work 1 dc in second ch from hook, 1 dc into the next 6[8] ch, work 2 dc into the end ch, work 1 dc into the reverse side of the remaining 7[9] ch, sl st into first dc (16[20] sts).

Round 2 (inc): 1 ch (does not count as a st), dc2inc, 1 dc in next 6[8] dc, (dc2inc) twice, 1 dc in next 6[8] dc, dc2inc, sl st into first dc (20[24] sts).

Round 3 (inc): 1 ch (does not count as a st), dc2inc, 1 dc in next 8[10] dc, (dc2inc) twice, 1 dc in next 8[10] dc, dc2inc, sl st into first dc (24[28] sts).

Round 4: 1 ch (does not count as a st), work 1 dc into each dc, sl st into first dc.

Duck bill
Adult size

Round 5 (inc): 1 ch (does not count as a st), dc2inc, 1 dc in next 10[12] dc, (dc2inc) twice, 1 dc in next 10[12] dc, dc2inc, sl st into first dc (28[32] sts).

Round 6: As round 4.

Round 7 (inc): 1 ch (does not count as a st), dc2inc, 1 dc in next 12[14] dc, (dc2inc) twice, 1 dc in next 12[14] dc, dc2inc, sl st into first dc (32[36] sts).

Round 8: As round 4.

Rep last round 0[2] more times.

Next (dec): 1 ch (does not count as a st), working into the back loop only of each stitch, (dc2dec) twice, 8[10] dc, (dc2dec) 4 times, 8[10] dc, (dc2dec) twice (24[28] sts). This will help to keep the back of the bill flat, making it easier to sew it to the hat. Fasten off, leaving a long length of yarn at the end.

MAKING UP
Bill

Stuff the bill, keeping a flattened shape. Sew together the 12[14] sts from each side of the opening. Attach the bill, positioning it over the rib and stitching the front loops of the decrease row to the main part.

Finishing touches

Weave in the ends of the yarn. Place the small black buttons over the larger white buttons and sew in place for the eyes.

LINING

See pages 142-5 for how to make and attach a cosy fleece or crocheted lining.

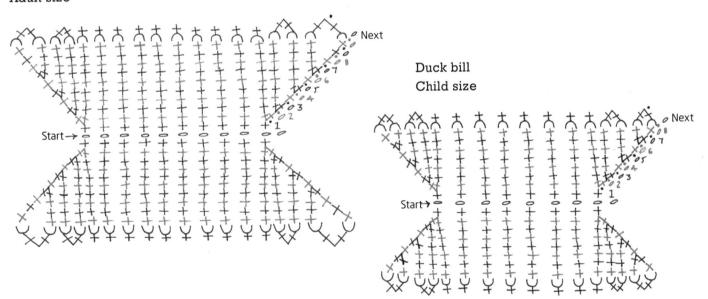

Duck bill
Child size

tiger

This project uses intarsia and different crochet stitches
to create the tiger stripes. For a less complicated
version, follow the instructions for the main piece
of the zebra with orange and black yarn.

MATERIALS

Wendy Mode Chunky, 50% wool, 50% acrylic
    (153yd/140m per 100g ball)
1[1] x 100g ball in 255 Blazing Orange (A)
1[1] x 100g ball in 220 Coal (B)
1[1] x 100g ball in 202 Vanilla (C)
Wendy Mode DK, 50% wool, 50% acrylic
    (155yd/142m per 50g ball)
1[1] x 50g ball in 220 Coal (D)
3mm (UK11:US-), 4.5mm (UK7:US7) and 5.5mm
    (UK5:USI/9) crochet hooks
2 x brown ¾[⅞]in (2[2.25]cm) diameter buttons
2 x black ½[⅝]in (1.25[1.5]cm) diameter buttons
Darning needle
Sewing needle
Black thread
Small amount of toy stuffing
Thin card to make tassels

SIZES

To fit: child, up to 20in (51cm) head circumference
[adult, up to 22in (56cm) head circumference]

TENSION

13 sts and 14 rows to 4in (10cm) over double
crochet on 5.5mm hook. Use larger or smaller hook
if necessary to obtain correct tension.

METHOD

The main part of the tiger hat is started off in rounds of double crochet, working two rounds of each colour to form the stripes. To shape the face, the hat is continued in rows. The white yarn is joined in with the black yarn to create the markings at the sides of the head, and the orange is used for the front of the face. The wavy stripes are formed by working two rows of double crochet, half treble and treble stitches over each other. The varying height of the stitches creates the wavy line. In the next two rows, the shorter stitches are worked over the longer ones. The cheeks, ears and nose are crocheted in rounds; they are shaped by increasing the stitches. The hat is finished off with button eyes and striped twisted cords with a big tassel attached to each one.

Main piece
Follow rounds 1 to 10 of chart for leopard hat on page 14

MAIN PIECE

Before you begin, wind 2 x 25g balls each of yarns B and C.

Both sizes

Starting at the top of the hat, with 5.5mm hook and A, make 4 ch and sl st to first ch to form a ring.

Rounds 1–8: Follow the pattern as for the zebra hat (see page 70), joining in B on round 3 and alternating the yarns every two rounds to create the stripes.

Round 9 (inc): With A, make 1 ch (does not count as a st), (dc2inc, 7 dc) 6 times, sl st into first dc (54 sts).

Round 10 (inc): 1 ch (does not count as a st), (dc2inc, 8 dc) 6 times, sl st into first dc (60 sts).

Child size only

Next: With B, make 1 ch (does not count as a st), work 1 dc in each dc, sl st into first dc.

Next: 3 ch (counts as first tr), (1 htr in next 2 sts, 1 dc in next 4 sts, 1 htr in next 2 sts, 1 tr in next 2 sts) 5 times, 1 htr in next 2 sts, 1 dc in next 4 sts, 1 htr in next 2 sts, 1 tr in next st, sl st into third of 3 ch. Fasten off B.

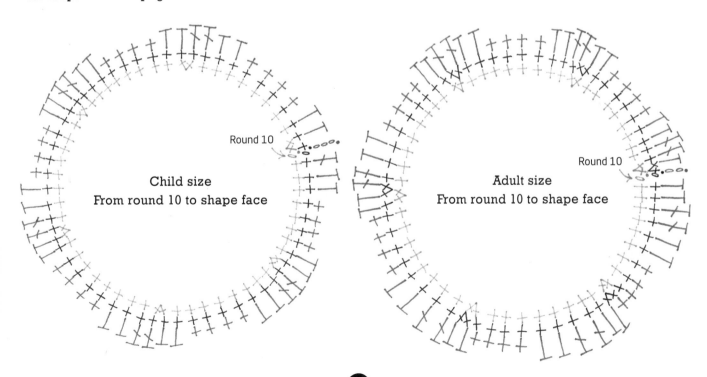

Round 10

Child size
From round 10 to shape face

Round 10

Adult size
From round 10 to shape face

Shape face

KEY

- ⟋ chain (ch)
- • slip stitch (sl st)
- + double crochet (dc)
- ⤬ dc2inc
- ⊤ half treble (htr)
- ⟊ treble (tr)
- ⟊ Adult size – treble (tr)
  Child size – make 3 chain (ch)
- ☐ Yarn A
- ☐ Yarn B
- ☐ Yarn C

Shape face

The following is worked in rows:

Row 1: With A, make 1 ch (does not count as a st), 1 dc in same st, 1 dc in next st, (1 htr in next 2 sts, 1 tr in next 2 sts, 1 htr in next 2 sts, 1 dc in next 4 sts) 5 times, 1 htr in next 2 sts, 1 tr in next 2 sts, 1 htr in next 2 sts, 1 dc in next 2 sts, turn.

Row 2: As row 1. Fasten off A. Join in C.

Row 3: With C, make 1 ch (does not count as a st), work 1 dc in next 23 sts, rejoin A and work 1 dc in next 14 sts, join in a new ball of C and work 1 dc in next 23 sts, turn.

Rejoin yarn B.

Row 4: With B, make 3 ch (counts as first tr), (1 htr in next 2 sts, 1 dc in next 4 sts, 1 htr in next 2 sts, 1 tr in next 2 sts) twice, 1 htr in next 2 sts, with A, work 1 dc in next 4 sts, 1 htr in next 2 sts, 1 tr in next 2 sts, 1 htr in next 2 sts, 1 dc in next 4 sts, join in a new ball of B and work (1 htr in next 2 sts, 1 tr in next 2 sts, 1 htr in next 2 sts, 1 dc in next 4 sts) twice, 1 htr in next 2 sts, 1 tr in next st, turn.

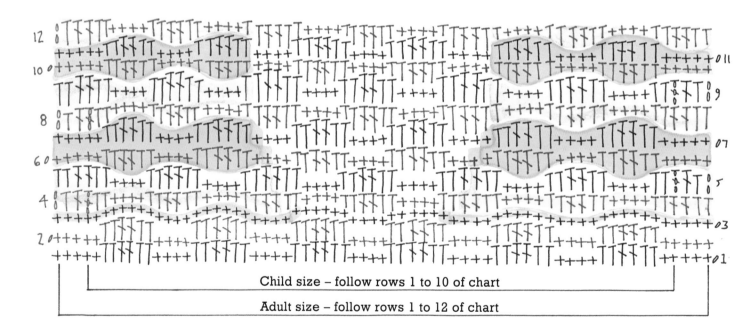

Child size – follow rows 1 to 10 of chart

Adult size – follow rows 1 to 12 of chart

Row 5: With B, make 3 ch (counts as first tr), (1 htr in next 2 sts, 1 dc in next 4 sts, 1 htr in next 2 sts, 1 tr in next 2 sts) twice, 1 htr in next st, with A, work 1 htr in next st, 1 dc in next 4 sts, 1 htr in next 2 sts, 1 tr in next 2 sts, 1 htr in next 2 sts, 1 dc in next 4 dc, 1 htr in next st, with B, work 1 htr in next st, (1 tr in next 2 sts, 1 htr in next 2 sts, 1 dc in next 4 sts, 1 htr in next 2 sts) twice, 1 tr in third of 3 ch, turn.

Row 6: With C, make 1 ch (does not count as a st), 1 dc in same st, (1 dc in next st, 1 htr in next 2 sts, 1 tr in next 2 sts, 1 htr in next 2 sts, 1 dc in next 3 sts) twice, with A, work 1 dc in next st, 1 htr in next 2 sts, 1 tr in next 2 sts, 1 htr in next 2 sts, 1 dc in next 4 sts, 1 htr in next 2 sts, 1 tr in next 2 sts, 1 htr in next 2 sts, 1 dc in next st, with C, work (1 dc in next 3 sts, 1 htr in next 2 sts, 1 tr in next 2 sts, 1 htr in next 2 sts, 1 dc in next st) twice, 1 dc in third of 3 ch, turn.

Row 7: With C, make 1 ch (does not count as a st), 1 dc in same st, 1 dc in next st, 1 htr in next 2 sts, 1 tr in next 2 sts, 1 htr in next 2 sts, 1 dc in next 4 sts, 1 htr in next 2 sts, 1 tr in next 2 sts, 1 htr in next 2 sts, 1 dc in next 2 sts, with A, work (1 dc in next 2 sts, 1 htr in next 2 sts, 1 tr in next 2 sts, 1 htr in next 2 sts, 1 dc in next 2 sts) twice, with C, work (1 dc in next 2 sts, 1 htr in next 2 sts, 1 tr in next 2 sts, 1 htr in next 2 sts, 1 dc in next 2 sts) twice, turn.

Row 8: With B, make 3 ch (counts as first tr), 1 htr in next 2 sts, 1 dc in next 4 sts, 1 htr in next 2 sts, 1 tr in next 2 sts, 1 htr in next 2 sts, 1 dc in next 4 sts, 1 htr in next 2 sts, with A, work (1 tr in next 2 sts, 1 htr in next 2 sts, 1 dc in next 4 dc, 1 htr in next 2 sts) twice, 1 tr in next 2 sts, with B, work 1 htr in next 2 sts, 1 dc in next 4 sts, 1 htr in next 2 sts, 1 tr in next 2 sts, 1 htr in next 2 sts, 1 dc in next 4 sts, 1 htr in next 2 sts, 1 tr in next st, turn.

Row 9: As row 8, finishing with 1 tr in third of 3 ch, turn. Fasten off B.

Row 10: With C, make 1 ch (does not count as a st), 1 dc in same st, 1 dc in next st, 1 htr in next 2 sts, 1 tr in next 2 sts, 1 htr in next 2 sts, 1 dc in next 4 sts, 1 htr in next 2 sts, 1 tr in next 2 sts, 1 htr in next 2 sts, with A, work (1 dc in next 4 sts, 1 htr in next 2 sts, 1 tr in next 2 sts, 1 htr in next 2 sts) twice, 1 dc in next 4 sts, with C, work 1 htr in next 2 sts, 1 tr in next 2 sts, 1 htr in next 2 sts, 1 dc in next 4 sts, 1 htr in next 2 sts, 1 tr in next 2 sts, 1 htr in next 2 sts, 1 dc in next st, 1 dc in third of 3 ch, turn.

Adult size only

Next (inc): With B, make 1 ch (does not count as a st), (dc2inc, 9 dc) 6 times, sl st into first dc (66 sts).

Next: 2 ch (counts as first htr), 1 htr in next st, (1 tr in next 2 sts, 1 htr in next 2 sts, 1 dc in next 4 sts, 1 htr in next 2 sts) 6 times, 1 tr in next 2 sts, 1 htr in next 2 sts, sl st into second of 2 ch. Fasten off B.

Shape face

The following is worked in rows:

Row 1: With A, make 1 ch (does not count as a st), 1 dc in same st, 1 dc in next 4 sts, (1 htr in next 2 sts, 1 tr in next 2 sts, 1 htr in next 2 sts, 1 dc in next 4 sts) 6 times, 1 dc in next st, turn.

Row 2: As row 1. Fasten off A. Join in C.

Row 3: With C, make 1 ch (does not count as a st), work 1 dc in next 26 sts, rejoin A and work 1 dc in next 14 sts, join in a new ball of C and work 1 dc in next 26 sts, turn.

Rejoin yarn B.

Row 4: With B, make 2 ch (counts as first htr), 1 htr in next st, (1 tr in next 2 sts, 1 htr in next 2 sts, 1 dc in next 4 sts, 1 htr in next 2 sts) twice, 1 tr in next 2 sts, 1 htr in next st, with A, work 1 htr in next st, 1 dc in next 4 sts, 1 htr in next 2 sts, 1 tr in next 2 sts, 1 htr in next 2 sts, 1 dc in next 4 sts, 1 htr in next st, join in a new ball of B and work 1 htr in next st, (1 tr in next 2 sts, 1 htr in next 2 sts, 1 dc in next 4 sts, 1 htr in next 2 sts) twice, 1 tr in next 2 sts, 1 htr in next 2 sts, turn.

Row 5: With B, make 2 ch (counts as first htr), 1 htr in next st, (1 tr in next 2 sts, 1 htr in next 2 sts, 1 dc in next 4 sts, 1 htr in next 2 sts) twice, 1 tr in next 2 sts, with A, work 1 htr in next 2 sts, 1 dc in next 4 sts, 1 htr in next 2 sts, 1 tr in next 2 sts, 1 htr in next 2 sts, 1 dc in next 4 sts, 1 htr in next 2 sts, with B, work (1 tr in next 2 sts, 1 htr in next 2 sts, 1 dc in next 4 sts, 1 htr in next 2 sts) twice, 1 tr in next 2 sts, 1 htr in next st, 1 htr in second of 2 ch, turn.

Row 6: With C, make 1 ch (does not count as a st), 1 dc in same st, (1 dc in next 4 sts, 1 htr in next 2 sts, 1 tr in next 2 sts, 1 htr in next 2 sts) twice, 1 dc in next 2 sts, with A, work 1 dc in next 2 sts, 1 htr in next 2 sts, 1 tr in next 2 sts, 1 htr in next 2 sts, 1 dc in next 4 sts, 1 htr in next 2 sts, 1 tr in next 2 sts, 1 htr in next 2 sts, 1 dc in next 2 sts, with C, work 1 dc in next 2 sts, (1 htr in next 2 sts, 1 tr in next 2 sts, 1 htr in next 2 sts, 1 dc in next 4 sts) twice, 1 dc in second of 2 ch, turn.

Row 7: With C, make 1 ch (does not count as a st), 1 dc in same st, (1 dc in next 4 sts, 1 htr in next 2 sts, 1 tr in next 2 sts, 1 htr in next 2 sts) twice, 1 dc in next st, with A, work 1 dc in next 3 sts, 1 htr in next 2 sts, 1 tr in next 2 sts, 1 htr in next 2 sts, 1 dc in next 4 sts, 1 htr in next 2 sts, 1 tr in next 2 sts, 1 htr in next 2 sts, 1 dc in next 3 sts, with C, work 1 dc in next st, (1 htr in next 2 sts, 1 tr in next 2 sts, 1 htr in next 2 sts, 1 dc in next 4 sts) twice, 1 dc in next dc, turn.

Row 8: With B, make 2 ch (counts as first htr), (1 htr in next st, 1 tr in next 2 sts, 1 htr in next 2 sts, 1 dc in next 4 sts, 1 htr in next st) twice, with A, work (1 htr in next st, 1 tr in next 2 sts, 1 htr in next 2 sts, 1 dc in next 4 dc, 1 htr in next st) twice, 1 htr in next st, 1 tr in next 2 sts, 1 htr in next st, with B, work (1 htr in next st, 1 dc in next 4 sts, 1 htr in next 2 sts, 1 tr in next 2 sts, 1 htr in next st) twice, 1 htr in next st, turn.

Row 9: As row 8, finishing with 1 htr in second of 2 ch, turn.

Row 10: With C, make 1 ch (does not count as a st), 1 dc in same st, (1 dc in next 4 sts, 1 htr in next 2 sts, 1 tr in next 2 sts, 1 htr in next 2 sts) twice, with A, work 1 dc in next 4 sts, (1 htr in next 2 sts, 1 tr in next 2 sts, 1 htr in next 2 sts, 1 dc in next 4 sts,) twice, with C, work (1 htr in next 2 sts, 1 tr in next 2 sts, 1 htr in next 2 sts, 1 dc in next 4 sts) twice, 1 dc in second of 2 ch, turn.

Row 11: As Row 10, finishing with 1 dc in last dc, turn. Fasten off C.

Row 12: As Row 8.

Both sizes
First earflap
Next: Starting at the centre back, with C [B], make 1 ch (does not count as a st), work 1 dc in next 5[6] sts. Do not turn. The following is worked in rows:

Adult size only
Row 1 (RS): With B, work 1 dc in next 15 sts, turn.

Row 2 (WS) (dec): Join in C and work 1 ch (does not count as a st), dc2dec, 1 dc in next 11 dc, dc2dec, turn, 1 ch (does not count as a st).

Both sizes
Next: With C, work 1 dc in next 13 dc, turn.

Join in B to child's size hat.

Next (dec): *With B, make 1 ch (does not count as a st), dc2dec, 1 dc in next 9 dc, dc2dec, turn (11 sts).

Next: With B, make 1 ch (does not count as a st), work 1 dc in each dc, turn.

Next (dec): With C, make 1 ch (does not count as a st), dc2dec, 1 dc in next 7 dc, dc2dec, turn (9 sts).

Next: With C, make 1 ch (does not count as a st), work 1 dc in each dc, turn.

Next (dec): With B, make 1 ch (does not count as a st), dc2dec, 1 dc in next 5 dc, dc2dec, turn (7 sts).

Next: With B, make 1 ch (does not count as a st), work 1 dc in each dc, turn.

Next (dec): With C, make 1 ch (does not count as a st), dc2dec, 1 dc in next 3 dc, dc2dec, turn (5 sts).

Next: With C, make 1 ch (does not count as a st), work 1 dc in each dc, turn.

Next (dec): With C, make 1 ch (does not count as a st), dc2dec, 1 dc in next 1 dc, dc2dec (3 sts).*

Fasten off.

Second earflap

Next: With right side facing, with yarn A, work 1 dc in each of the 24 sts across the front of the hat. Do not turn.

The following is worked in rows:

Adult size only

Row 1 (RS): With B, work 1 dc in next 15 sts, turn.

Row 2 (WS) (dec): Join in C and work 1 ch (does not count as a st), dc2dec, 1 dc in next 11 sts, dc2dec, turn, 1 ch (does not count as a st).

Both sizes

Next: With C, work 1 dc in next 13 dc, turn.

Next: Work from * to * of first earflap. Fasten off.

Earflap facings (make 2)

Omit if you plan to add a crocheted lining.

Both sizes

With 5.5mm hook and A, follow the earflap facing pattern as for the leopard hat on page 18.

Edging

With 4.5mm hook and A, follow edging pattern for the earflap facing on page 18.

EARS (MAKE 2)

Both sizes

With 5.5mm hook and A, follow the ear pattern as for the leopard hat on page 19.

NOSE

Both sizes

With 3mm hook and D, follow the nose pattern as for the leopard hat on page 20.

CHEEKS (MAKE 2)

Both sizes

With 5.5mm hook and C, follow the cheek pattern as for the rabbit hat on page 137.

MAKING UP

Edging

Sew together the back seam of the hat. With right side of work facing, using 4.5mm hook and A, rejoin yarn to the back of the hat by the second earflap and follow the edging pattern as for the leopard hat on page 23.

Ears

Finish the ears as for the leopard hat on page 23.

Cheeks

Sew the cheeks to the face, around ⅝in (1.5cm) from the lower edge, setting them close together.

Nose

Flatten the nose and sew the 12[16] stitches from each side of the top edge together. Sew the nose to the centre front of the hat, with the stitched edge in line with the top shaping of the cheeks.

Finishing touches

If making a crocheted lining, attach the twisted cords to the hat after inserting the lining. Weave in all the yarn ends. Place the small black buttons over the larger brown buttons and sew in place for the eyes. Make two 8[12]in (20[30]cm)-long striped twisted cords (see page 154) using 3[4] strands each of yarn A and B. Make two tassels (see page 155) measuring 4[5⅛]in (10[13]cm) long in B, and attach each to one end of the twisted cord, then stitch the other end of the cord to the tip of the earflap.

LINING

See pages 142–5 for how to make and attach a cosy fleece or crocheted lining.

husky

After a snowfall, an exciting day of sledging
calls for warm accessories, such as this husky
hat in grey and white yarn with cute ears,
twisted cords and pompoms.

MATERIALS

King Cole Big Value Chunky, 100% acrylic
(167yd/152m per 100g ball)
2[2] x 100g balls in 547 Grey (A)
1[1] x 100g ball in 822 White (B)
Oddment of chunky yarn in black (C)
4.5mm (UK7:US7), 5mm (UK6:USH/8) and 6mm
(UK4:USJ/10) crochet hooks
2 x blue ¾[⅞]in (2[2.25]cm) diameter buttons
2 x black ½[⅝]in (1.25[1.5]cm) diameter buttons
Darning needle
Sewing needle
Black thread
Small amount of toy stuffing
Thin card to make pompoms

SIZES

To fit: child, up to 20in (51cm) head circumference
[adult, up to 22in (56cm) head circumference]

TENSION

13 sts and 14 rows to 4in (10cm) over double
crochet on 6mm hook. Use larger or smaller hook
if necessary to obtain correct tension.

METHOD

The main piece is started in rounds and the stitches increased to shape the crown. The face shaping is crocheted in rows in two shades of yarn. The unused yarn is carried across the back of the work for the first few rows of the face shaping. Another ball of the main shade is joined in to finish the remainder of the face. The muzzle is crocheted using a smaller hook. The nose is worked in rows and the stitches are increased at each end to form the triangular shape. The ears are in two pieces, which are joined by crocheting the edges of them together to form an edging. They are stuffed lightly and shaped with a few stitches before sewing them to the hat. Button eyes, twisted cords and pompoms finish the husky.

MAIN PIECE

Both sizes

Starting at the top of the hat, with 6mm hook and A, follow the pattern for the leopard hat main piece on page 14 to the end of round 10[11].

Both sizes

Next: 1 ch (does not count as a st), work 1 dc in each dc, sl st into first dc.
Rep last row 2 more times.

KEY

- ✐ chain (ch)
- • slip stitch (sl st)
- + double crochet (dc)
- ✕✕ dc2inc
- ✕✕ dc2dec
- ☐ Yarn A
- ▨ Yarn B

Shape face

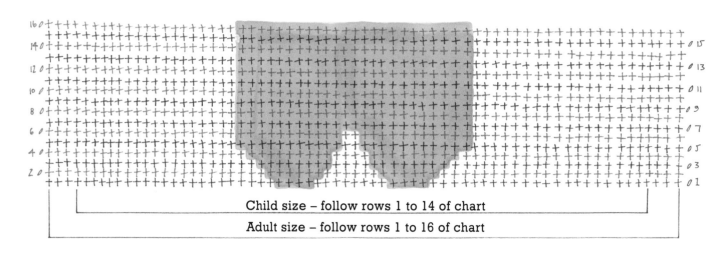

Child size – follow rows 1 to 14 of chart
Adult size – follow rows 1 to 16 of chart

Shape face

When working rows 1 to 6, carry unused yarn across the back of the centre 24 stitches (see Joining in colours, page 153). The following is worked in rows:

Row 1: 1 ch (does not count as a st), work 1 dc in next 22[25] dc, join in B and work 1 dc in next 4 dc, with A, work 1 dc in next 8 dc, with B, work 1 dc in next 4 dc, with A, work 1 dc in next 22[25] dc, turn.

Row 2: With A, make 1 ch (does not count as a st), work 1 dc in next 21[24] dc, with B, work 1 dc in next 6 dc, with A, work 1 dc in next 6 dc, with B, work 1 dc in next 6 dc, with A, work 1 dc in next 21[24] dc, turn.

Row 3: With A, make 1 ch (does not count as a st), work 1 dc in next 20[23] dc, with B, work 1 dc in next 8 dc, with A, work 1 dc in next 4 dc, with B, work 1 dc in next 8 dc, with A, work 1 dc in next 20[23] dc, turn.

Row 4: With A, make 1 ch (does not count as a st), work 1 dc in next 19[22] dc, with B, work 1 dc in next 9 dc, with A, work 1 dc in next 4 dc, with B, work 1 dc in next 9 dc, with A, work 1 dc in next 19[22] dc, turn.

Rows 5-6: With A, make 1 ch (does not count as a st), work 1 dc in next 18[21] dc, with B, work 1 dc in next 11 dc, with A, work 1 dc in next 2 dc, with B, work 1 dc in next 11 dc, with A, work 1 dc in next 18[21] dc, turn.

Row 7: With A, make 1 ch (does not count as a st), work 1 dc in next 18[21] dc, with B, work 1 dc in next 24 dc, join in the second ball of yarn A and work 1 dc in next 18[21] dc in A, turn.

Rows 8-14[16]: With A, make 1 ch (does not count as a st), work 1 dc in next 18[21] dc, with B, work 1 dc in next 24 dc, with A, work 1 dc in next 18[21] dc, turn.

First earflap

With 6mm hook and A, follow the pattern for the first earflap on the leopard hat on page 16.

Second earflap

Next: With right side facing and yarn B, work 1 dc in each of the 24 dc across the front of the hat.

Rejoin and continue in yarn A, following the pattern for the second earflap on the leopard hat on page 16.

Earflap facings (make 2)

Omit if you plan to add a crocheted lining.

Both sizes

With 6mm hook and A, follow the earflap facing pattern as for the leopard hat on page 18.

Edging

With 5mm hook and A, follow edging pattern for the earflap facing on page 18.

EARS (MAKE 2)

Both sizes

With 6mm hook and B, make 2 ch.

*Row 1: Work 3 dc into second ch from hook, turn (3 sts).

Row 2 (inc): 1 ch (does not count as a st), dc2inc, 1 dc, dc2inc, turn (5 sts).

Row 3 (inc): 1 ch (does not count as a st), dc2inc, 1 dc in next 3 dc, dc2inc, turn (7 sts).

Row 4 (inc): 1 ch (does not count as a st), dc2inc, 1 dc in next 5 dc, dc2inc, turn (9 sts).

Row 5 (inc): 1 ch (does not count as a st), dc2inc, 1 dc in next 7 dc, dc2inc, turn (11 sts).

Row 6 (inc): 1 ch (does not count as a st), dc2inc, 1 dc in next 9 dc, dc2inc, turn (13 sts).

Adult size only

Next (inc): 1 ch (does not count as a st), dc2inc, 1 dc in next 11 dc, dc2inc, turn (15 sts).

Next (inc): 1 ch (does not count as a st), dc2inc, 1 dc in next 13 dc, dc2inc, turn (17 sts).

Both sizes

Next: 1 ch (does not count as a st), work 1 dc in each dc, turn.

Rep last row 5 more times.*

Fasten off, leaving a long length of yarn at the end.

Edging

With 5mm hook, rejoin yarn A to the edge of the last row. **Work 1 dc into each stitch up the edge of the next 12[14] rows, work 3 dc into the ch at the tip of the ear, 1 dc into each stitch down the edge of the next 12[14] rows.** Fasten off. This will be the inner ear.

To make the outer ear piece, with 6mm hook and A, make 2 ch. Rep from * to *. Do not fasten off.

Change to 5mm hook and work from ** to ** to complete the first row of edging, turn.

Join ear pieces

Place the two ear pieces together with the inner ear facing up. With 5mm hook and A, working into the stitches of the inner and outer ear pieces at the same time to join, make 1 ch, work 1 dc into each of the next 13[15] dc, dc2inc, 1 dc into each of the next 13[15] dc. Fasten off, leaving a length of yarn at the end.

Ears
Child size

Join ear pieces - work into both ear pieces at the same time to join

Ears
Adult size

Join ear pieces - work into both ear pieces at the same time to join

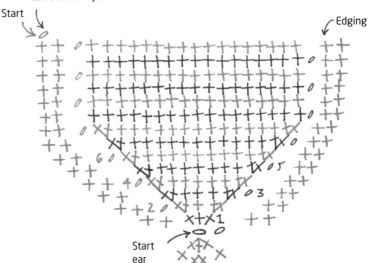

MUZZLE
Both sizes
With 4.5mm hook and B, make 4 ch and sl st to first ch to form a ring. Follow the muzzle pattern for the deer on page 46.

NOSE
Both sizes
With 4.5mm hook and C, make 2 ch.
Row 1: Work 3 dc into second ch from hook, turn (3 sts).
Row 2: 1 ch (does not count as a st), work 1 dc in each dc, turn.
Row 3 (inc): 1 ch (does not count as a st), dc2inc, 1 dc, dc2inc, turn (5 sts).
Adult size only
Row 4 (inc): 1 ch (does not count as a st), dc2inc, 1 dc in next 3 dc, dc2inc, turn (7 sts).
Both sizes
Fasten off, leaving a long length of yarn at the end.

Nose
Child size – work rows 1 to 3
Adult size – work rows 1 to 4

MAKING UP
Edging
Sew together the back seam of the hat. With right side of work facing, using 5mm hook and B, rejoin yarn to the back of the hat by the second earflap and follow the edging pattern as for the leopard hat on page 23.

Ears
Push a thin layer of stuffing into the ears. With the length of yarn left after fastening off the edging, sew the lower edges of the inner and outer pieces together. Bring the two corners of each side from the lower edge of the ear to the middle to shape and stitch to hold in place. Sew the ears to the main section of the hat, stitching all around the lower edges to keep them securely in place.

Muzzle and nose
Use the long length of yarn left after fastening off to stitch the muzzle to the front of the hat, positioning it just above the edging, leaving a small opening. Push some stuffing into the opening to shape the muzzle before stitching it down. Use the length of yarn after fastening off the nose to sew it in place just above the centre of the muzzle, with the wider edge at the top.

Finishing touches
If making a crocheted lining, attach the twisted cords to the hat after inserting the lining. Weave in all the yarn ends. Place the small black buttons over the larger blue buttons and sew in place for the eyes. Make two twisted cords (see page 154) measuring 8[12]in (20[30]cm) long in A, using 6[8] strands of yarn. Make two 2[2⅜]in (5[6]cm) pompoms (see page 155) in B and attach each to one end of the twisted cord, then stitch the other end of the cord to the tip of the earflap.

LINING
See pages 142–5 for how to make and attach a cosy fleece or crocheted lining.

bear

This bear hat has a lovely cuddly quality using a combination of brushed and textured yarns in matching shades of brown. You could substitute brown for white to make a polar bear.

MATERIALS

Lion Brand Jiffy, 100% acrylic (135yd/123m per 85g ball)

2[2] x 85g balls in 126 Espresso (A)

Lion Brand Homespun, 98% acrylic, 2% polyester (185yd/169m per 170g ball)

1[1] x 170g ball in 601 Desert Mountain (B)

Oddment of chunky yarn in black (C)

4.5mm (UK7:US7) and 5.5mm (UK5:US1/9) crochet hooks

2 x brown ¾[⅞]in (2[2.25]cm) diameter buttons

2 x black ½[⅝]in (1.25[1.5]cm) diameter buttons

Darning needle

Sewing needle

Black thread

Small amount of toy stuffing

Thin card to make pompoms

SIZES

To fit: child, up to 20in (51cm) head circumference [adult, up to 22in (56cm) head circumference]

TENSION

13 sts and 14 rows to 4in (10cm) over double crochet on 5.5mm hook. Use larger or smaller hook if necessary to obtain correct tension.

METHOD

The main piece is worked in rounds of double crochet with the earflaps crocheted in rows. The ears are made in one piece and crocheted in a spherical shape, starting with the textured yarn forming the back of the ear, and then changing halfway through to the main yarn to form the inside of the ear. The ears are flattened, stuffed lightly and stitched at the lower ends to shape them. The muzzle is crocheted in rounds to form a bowl shape, which is stitched to the face, stuffed and finished with the crocheted button nose. Button eyes and big pompoms to match the ears, on the ends of twisted cords, complete the hat.

MAIN PIECE

Both sizes

Starting at the top of the hat, with 5.5mm hook and A, follow the pattern for the leopard hat main piece on page 14.

Earflap facings (make 2)

Omit if you plan to add a crocheted lining.

Both sizes

With 5.5mm hook and A, follow the earflap facing pattern as for the leopard hat on page 18.

Edging

With 4.5mm hook and A, follow edging pattern for the earflap facing on page 18.

EARS (MAKE 2)

Both sizes

Starting at the centre of the back of the ear, with 5.5mm hook and B, make 4 ch and sl st to first ch to form a ring.

Round 1: 1 ch (does not count as a st), work 5 dc into ring, sl st into first dc (5 sts).

Round 2 (inc): 1 ch (does not count as a st), (dc2inc) 5 times, sl st into first dc (10 sts).

Round 3 (inc): 1 ch (does not count as a st), (dc2inc, 1 dc) 5 times, sl st into first dc (15 sts).

Round 4 (inc): 1 ch (does not count as a st), (dc2inc, 2 dc) 5 times, sl st into first dc (20 sts).

Round 5 (inc): 1 ch (does not count as a st), (dc2inc, 3 dc) 5 times, sl st into first dc (25 sts).

Round 6 (inc): 1 ch (does not count as a st), (dc2inc, 4 dc) 5 times, sl st into first dc (30 sts).

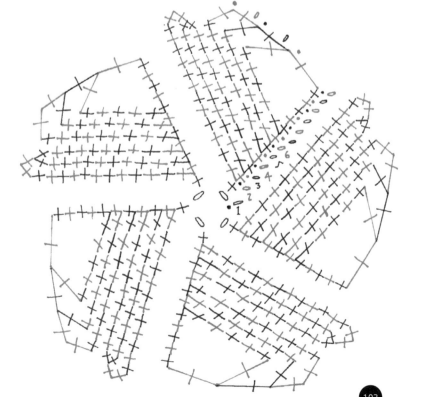

Ear
Adult size
Child size – follow chart to end of round 6

KEY

⚬ chain (ch)
• slip stitch (sl st)
+ double crochet (dc)
XX dc2inc
Xx dc2dec

Adult size only

Next (inc): 1 ch (does not count as a st), (dc2inc, 5 dc) 5 times, sl st into first dc (35 sts).

Both sizes

Next: 1 ch (does not count as a st), work 1 dc in each dc, sl st into first dc.

Next: Rep last round 2 more times. Join in and continue in yarn A.

Inner ear

Next: 1 ch (does not count as a st), work 1 dc in each dc, sl st into first dc.

Adult size only

Next (dec): 1 ch (does not count as a st), (dc2dec, 5 dc) 5 times, sl st into first dc (30 sts).

Both sizes

Next (dec): 1 ch (does not count as a st), (dc2dec, 1 dc) 10 times, sl st into first dc (20 sts).

Next (dec): 1 ch (does not count as a st), (dc2dec) 10 times, sl st into first dc (10 sts).

Finishing at the centre front of the inner ear, fasten off, leaving a long length of yarn at the end.

MUZZLE

Both sizes

With 5.5mm hook and A, make 4 ch and sl st to first ch to form a ring.

Round 1: 1 ch (does not count as a st), work 6 dc into ring, sl st into first dc (6 sts).

Round 2 (inc): 1 ch (does not count as a st), (dc2inc) 6 times, sl st into first dc (12 sts).

Round 3 (inc): 1 ch (does not count as a st), (dc2inc, 1 dc) 6 times, sl st into first dc (18 sts).

Round 4 (inc): 1 ch (does not count as a st), (dc2inc, 2 dc) 6 times, sl st into first dc (24 sts).

Child size only

Next: 1 ch (does not count as a st), work 1 dc in each dc, sl st into first dc.

Ear
Child size – round
6 to end

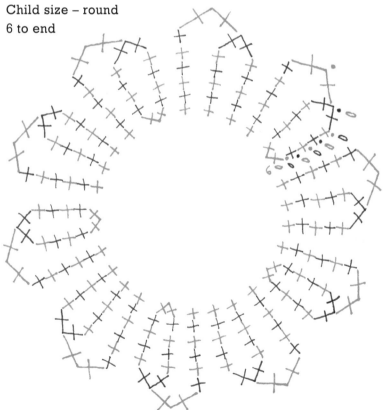

Muzzle
Child size

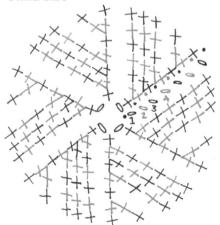

Both sizes
Next: 1 ch (does not count as a st),
(dc2inc, 3 dc) 6 times, sl st into first dc
(30 sts).
Next: 1 ch (does not count as a st), work
1 dc in each dc, sl st into first dc.
Adult size only
Next: 1 ch (does not count as a st),
(dc2inc, 4 dc) 6 times, sl st into first dc
(36 sts).
Next: 1 ch (does not count as a st), work
1 dc in each dc, sl st into first dc.
Fasten off, leaving a long length of yarn
at the end.

NOSE
Both sizes
With 4.5mm hook and C, make 4 ch and
sl st to first ch to form a ring.
Round 1: 1 ch (does not count as
a st), work 6 dc into ring, sl st into first
dc (6 sts).
Round 2 (inc): 1 ch (does not count
as a st), (dc2inc) 6 times, sl st into first
dc (12 sts).
Adult size only
Next: 1 ch (does not count as a st), (dc2inc,
1 dc) 6 times, sl st into first dc (18 sts).

Both sizes
Next: 1 ch (does not count as a st), work
1 dc in each dc, sl st into first dc.
Next: Rep last round once more.
Adult size only
Next (dec): 1 ch (does not count as a st),
(dc2dec, 1 dc) 6 times, sl st into first dc
(12 sts).
Both sizes
Next: 1 ch (does not count as a st), work
1 dc in each dc, sl st into first dc.
Fasten off, leaving a long length of yarn
at the end.

Muzzle
Adult size

Nose
Child size

Nose
Adult size

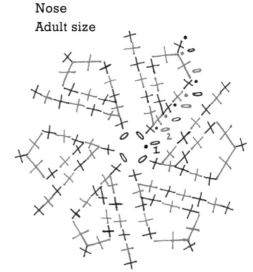

MAKING UP
Edging
With right side of work facing, using 4.5mm hook and A, rejoin yarn to the back of the hat by the second earflap and follow the edging pattern as for the leopard hat on page 23.

Ears
Fill the ears lightly with toy stuffing and, using a darning needle, weave the long length through the stitches of the last round. Pull on the yarn to gather and close the opening before securing with a few stitches worked over each other. To shape the ear, fold it in half with yarn B on the outside and sew a few stitches, around 1[1½]in (2.5[4]cm) from the lower edge of the fold, to hold the shaping in place. Push the excess of the curve at the folded end at the back of the ear, up inside the ear shaping (**see 1**) so it forms an even lower edge and stitch to hold in place (**see 2**). Sew the ears to the top of the hat, stitching all around the lower edges to hold them firmly in position.

Muzzle and nose
Use the long length of yarn left after fastening off to stitch the muzzle to the front of the hat, positioning it just above the edging, leaving a small opening. Push some stuffing into the opening to shape the muzzle before stitching it down. Weave the length of yarn left after fastening off the nose through the last round of stitches. Pull the yarn to gather the opening and stitch securely. This will produce a flattened, round button-shaped nose. Sew the nose in place, just above the centre of the muzzle.

Finishing touches
If making a crocheted lining, attach the twisted cords to the hat after inserting the lining. Place the small black buttons over the larger brown buttons and sew in place for the eyes. Weave in all the yarn ends. Make two twisted cords (see page 154) using A, each measuring 8[12]in (20[30]cm) long, using 6[8] strands of yarn. Make two 2[2⅜]in (5[6]cm) pompoms (see page 155) in B and attach each to one end of the twisted cord, then stitch the other end of the cord to the tip of the earflap.

LINING
See pages 142–5 for how to make and attach a cosy fleece or crocheted lining.

Making up ear

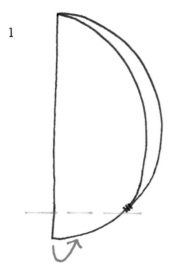

1

2

Push the excess of the curve inside the ear shaping to form an even lower edge

pig

It's a classic pink pig! For a variation on this style,
crocheted in a uniform colour, you could substitute
one ball of yarn for a lighter or darker shade of pink
to finish the edging, cords and tassels.

MATERIALS

Bergère de France Duvetine, 73% acrylic,
19% polyamide, 8% polyester (76yd/70m
per 50g ball)

4[4] x 50g balls in 24609 Petale (A)

4mm (UK8:USG/6) and 5mm (UK6:USH/8) crochet
hooks

2 x white ¾[⅞]in (2[2.25]cm) diameter buttons

2 x black ½[⅝]in (1.25[1.5]cm) diameter buttons

2 x black ½in (1.25cm) diameter buttons for nostrils

Darning needle

Sewing needle

Black thread

Small amount of toy stuffing

Thin card to make tassels

SIZES

To fit: child, up to 20in (51cm) head circumference
[adult, up to 22in (56cm) head circumference]

TENSION

13 sts and 14 rows to 4in (10cm) over double
crochet on 5mm hook. Use larger or smaller hook
if necessary to obtain correct tension.

METHOD

The ears, snout and main part of the pig hat are worked in rounds of double crochet. The ears are lightly stuffed and attached to the hat. The flattened shape of the snout is formed by crocheting into just the back loops of the stitches at the beginning and end rows of the side edges. Buttons are stitched and pulled into the snout to shape it further after stuffing the piece. Button eyes, twisted cords and tassels finish the hat.

MAIN PIECE

Both sizes

Starting at the top of the hat, with 5mm hook and A, follow the pattern for the leopard hat main piece on page 14.

Earflap facings (make 2)

Omit if you plan to add a crocheted lining.

Both sizes

With 5mm hook and A, follow the earflap facing pattern as for the leopard hat on page 18.

Edging

With 4mm hook and A, follow edging pattern for the earflap facing on page 18.

EARS (MAKE 2)

Both sizes

Starting at the top of the ear, with 5mm hook and A, make 4 ch and sl st to first ch to form a ring.

Round 1: 1 ch (does not count as a st), work 6 dc into ring, sl st into first dc (6 sts).

Round 2 (inc): 1 ch (does not count as a st), (dc2inc) 6 times, sl st into first dc (12 sts).

Round 3: 1 ch (does not count as a st), work 1 dc in each dc, sl st into first dc.

Round 4 (inc): 1 ch (does not count as a st), (dc2inc, 1 dc) 6 times, sl st into first dc (18 sts).

Ear
Adult size
Child size – follow chart
to end of round 6

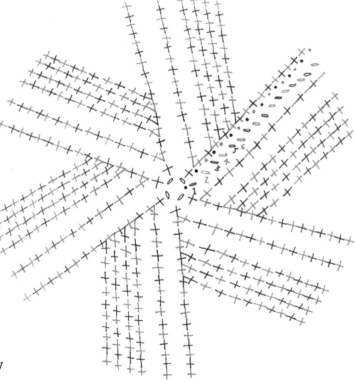

KEY

- ⌀ chain (ch)
- • slip stitch (sl st)
- + double crochet (dc)
- ⤬⤬ dc2inc
- ⤬ dc2dec
- ⟂ double crochet into back loop only

Ear
Child size
Round 6 to end

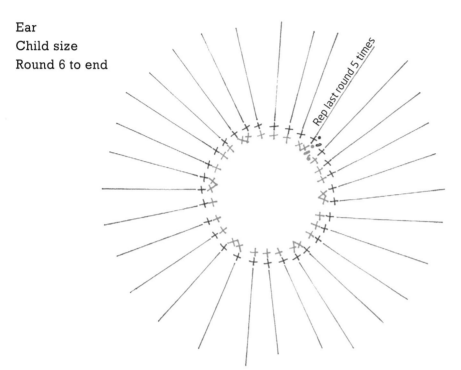

Rep last round 5 times

Round 5 (inc): 1 ch (does not count as a st), (dc2inc, 2 dc) 6 times, sl st into first dc (24 sts).

Round 6 (inc): 1 ch (does not count as a st), (dc2inc, 3 dc) 6 times, sl st into first dc (30 sts).

Adult size only
Next (inc): 1 ch (does not count as a st), (dc2inc, 4 dc) 6 times, sl st into first dc (36 sts).

Both sizes
Next: 1 ch (does not count as a st), work 1 dc in each dc, sl st into first dc.
Rep last round 5[8] more times.
Fasten off, leaving a long length of yarn at the end.

SNOUT
Both sizes
Starting at the centre of the snout, with 5mm hook and A, make 4 ch and sl st to first ch to form a ring.

Round 1: 1 ch (does not count as a st), work 5 dc into ring, sl st into first dc (5 sts).

Round 2 (inc): 1 ch (does not count as a st), (dc2inc) 5 times, sl st into first dc (10 sts).

Round 3 (inc): 1 ch (does not count as a st), (dc2inc, 1 dc) 5 times, sl st into first dc (15 sts).

Round 4 (inc): 1 ch (does not count as a st), (dc2inc, 2 dc) 5 times, sl st into first dc (20 sts).

Round 5 (inc): 1 ch (does not count as a st), (dc2inc, 3 dc) 5 times, sl st into first dc (25 sts).

Adult size only
Next (inc): 1 ch (does not count as a st), (dc2inc, 4 dc) 5 times, sl st into first dc (30 sts).

Both sizes
Next: 1 ch (does not count as a st), work 1 dc into the back loop only of each dc, sl st into first dc. This will help to keep the front of the snout flat.

Next: 1 ch (does not count as a st), work 1 dc in each dc, sl st into first dc.
Rep last round 1[2] more times.

Next: 1 ch (does not count as a st), work 1 dc into the back loop only of each dc, sl st into first dc.

Adult size only
Next (dec): 1 ch (does not count as a st), (dc2dec, 4 dc) 5 times, sl st into first dc (25 sts).

Both sizes
Next (dec): 1 ch (does not count as a st), (dc2dec, 3 dc) 5 times, sl st into first dc (20 sts).

Next (dec): 1 ch (does not count as a st), (dc2dec, 2 dc) 5 times, sl st into first dc (15 sts).

Fasten off, leaving a long length of yarn at the end.

Snout
Adult size
Child size –
follow chart to
end of round 5

Snout
Child size
Round 5 to end

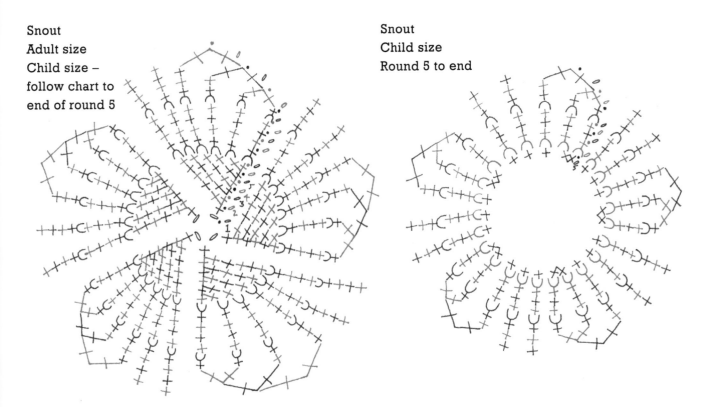

MAKING UP
Edging
With right side of work facing, using 4mm hook and A, rejoin yarn to the back of the hat by the second earflap and follow the edging pattern as for the leopard hat on page 23.

Ears
Stuff the ears lightly, keeping a flattened shape. With the long length of yarn left, sew the 15[18] stitches together from each side of the last round of the ears to join, forming a straight edge. Shape the ears by bringing the two corners to the middle and stitch together to hold in place. Sew the ears to the main section

of the hat, stitching all around the lower edges to prevent them from flopping over.

Snout
Stuff the snout, keeping the front flat. With the long length of yarn left at the end, run a line of stitches through the last round and pull the yarn to gather the stitches and close the opening before fastening off. Sew the small buttons to the snout, stitching right through to the back of the work and pulling tight on the thread to draw the nostrils in. Attach the snout to the main part of the hat at the centre front, positioning it just above the edging stitches.

Finishing touches
If making a crocheted lining, attach the twisted cords to the hat after inserting the lining. Weave in all yarn ends. Make two twisted cords (see page 154) measuring 8[12]in (20[30]cm) long in A, using 6[8] strands of yarn. Make two tassels (see page 155) measuring 4[5⅛]in (10[13]cm) long in A, and attach each to one end of the cord, then stitch the other end of the cord to the tip of the earflap. Place the small black buttons over the larger white buttons and sew in place for the eyes.

LINING
See pages 142–5 for how to make and attach a cosy fleece or crocheted lining.

giraffe

For this hat, the distinctive giraffe markings are made
with crocheted polygon patches worked in various sizes,
while the giant tassels at the end of the cords
represent the giraffe's tail.

MATERIALS

Bergère de France Magic +, 50% worsted wool,
  50% acrylic (87yd/80m per 50g ball)
2[3] x 50g balls in 23308 Brebis (A)
Bergère de France Toison, 77% acrylic, 20%
  worsted wool, 3% polyamide (76yd/70m per
  50g ball)
1[1] x 50g ball in 24539 Muscade (B)
Bergère de France Sport, 51% worsted wool, 49%
  acrylic (98yd/90m per 50g ball)
1[1] x 50g ball in 22342 Campeche (C)
3mm (UK11:US-), 4.5mm (UK7:US7), 5mm
  (UK6:USH/8) and 6mm (UK4:USJ/10) crochet
  hooks
2 x brown ¾[⅞]in (2[2.25]cm) diameter buttons
2 x black ½[⅝]in (1.25[1.5]cm) diameter buttons
Darning needle
Sewing needle
Black thread
Small amount of toy stuffing
Thin card to make tassels

SIZES

To fit: child, up to 20in (51cm) head circumference
[adult, up to 22in (56cm) head circumference]

TENSION

13 sts and 14 rows to 4in (10cm) over double
crochet on 6mm hook. Use larger or smaller hook
if necessary to obtain correct tension.

METHOD

The majority of the hat is worked in double crochet. The nose is crocheted using a smaller hook to produce a denser fabric. The nose and the horn-like ossicones are all filled firmly with toy stuffing. A thin layer of stuffing is also pushed into the ears, which are folded at one corner to shape them before attaching them to the hat. The markings are polygon-shaped patches, crocheted in treble and chain stitches and sewn around the hat to form the patterned coat of the giraffe.

MAIN PIECE
Both sizes

Starting at the top of the hat, with 6mm hook and A, follow the pattern for the leopard hat main piece on page 14.

EARFLAP FACINGS (MAKE 2)

Omit if you plan to add a crocheted lining.
Both sizes

With 6mm hook and A, follow the earflap facing pattern as for the leopard hat on page 18.
Edging

With 5mm hook and A, follow edging pattern for the earflap facing on page 18.

EARS (MAKE 2)
Both sizes

Starting at the top of the ear, with 6mm hook and A, make 4 ch and sl st to first ch to form a ring.

Round 1: 1 ch (does not count as a st), work 6 dc into ring, sl st into first dc (6 sts).

Round 2: 1 ch (does not count as a st), work 1 dc in each dc, sl st into first dc.

Round 3 (inc): 1 ch (does not count as a st), (dc2inc) 6 times, sl st into first dc (12 sts).

Round 4: As round 2.

Round 5 (inc): 1 ch (does not count as a st), (dc2inc, 1 dc) 6 times, sl st into first dc (18 sts).

Round 6: As round 2.

Round 7 (inc): 1 ch (does not count as a st), (dc2inc, 2 dc) 6 times, sl st into first dc (24 sts).

Round 8: As round 2.

Ear
Adult size
Child size –
follow chart
to end of
round 8

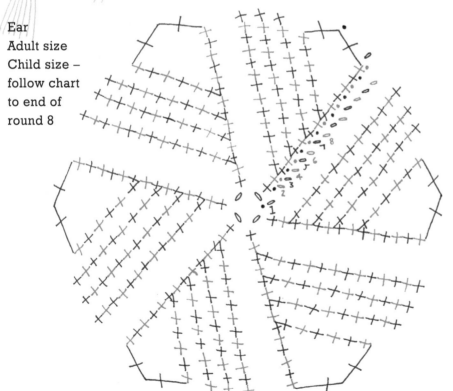

KEY
- ⟋ chain (ch)
- • slip stitch (sl st)
- ✛ double crochet (dc)
- ✕✕ dc2inc
- ✕✕ dc2dec
- ⊤ half treble (htr)
- � treble (tr)

Ear
Child size
Round 8 to end

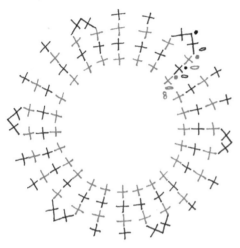

Adult size only
Next (inc): 1 ch (does not count as a st),
(dc2inc, 3 dc) 6 times, sl st into first dc
(30 sts).
Both sizes
Next: As round 2.
Rep last round 1[4] more times.
Next (dec): 1 ch (does not count as a st),
(dc2dec, 2[3] dc) 6 times, sl st into first dc
(18[24] sts).
Fasten off, leaving a long length of yarn
at the end.

OSSICONES (MAKE 2)

Starting at the top of the ossicone, with
6mm hook and B, make 4 ch and sl st to
first ch to form a ring.
Round 1: 1 ch (does not count as a st),
work 5[6] dc into ring, sl st into first dc
(5[6] sts).
Round 2 (inc): 1 ch (does not count as a
st), (dc2inc) 5[6] times, sl st into first dc
(10[12] sts).
Round 3: 1 ch (does not count as a st),
work 1 dc in each dc, sl st into first dc.
Rep last round once[twice] more.
Join in yarn A and change to 4.5mm hook.
Next: As round 3.
Rep last round 5[10] more times.
Fasten off, leaving a long length of yarn
A at the end.

Ossicones
Child size

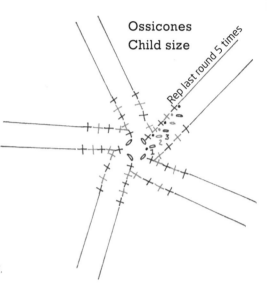

Ossicones
Adult size

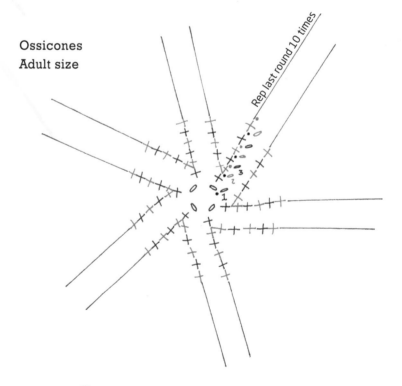

NOSE

With 4.5mm hook and A, make 4 ch and join with a sl st to the first ch to form a ring.

Round 1: 1 ch (does not count as a st), work 6 dc into ring, sl st to first dc (6 sts).

Round 2 (inc): 1 ch (does not count as a st), (dc2inc) 6 times, sl st into first dc (12 sts).

Round 3 (inc): 1 ch (does not count as a st), (dc2inc, 1 dc) 6 times, sl st into first dc (18 sts).

Round 4 (inc): 1 ch (does not count as a st), (dc2inc, 2 dc) 6 times, sl st into first dc (24 sts).

Adult size only

Next (inc): 1 ch (does not count as a st), (dc2inc, 3 dc) 6 times, sl st into first dc (30 sts).

Both sizes

Next round: 1 ch (does not count as a st), work 1 dc in each dc, sl st to first dc.
Rep last round 5[7] more times.
Fasten off, leaving a long length of yarn at the end.

Nose
Adult size
Child size –
follow chart to
end of round 4

Nose
Child size – round 4 to end

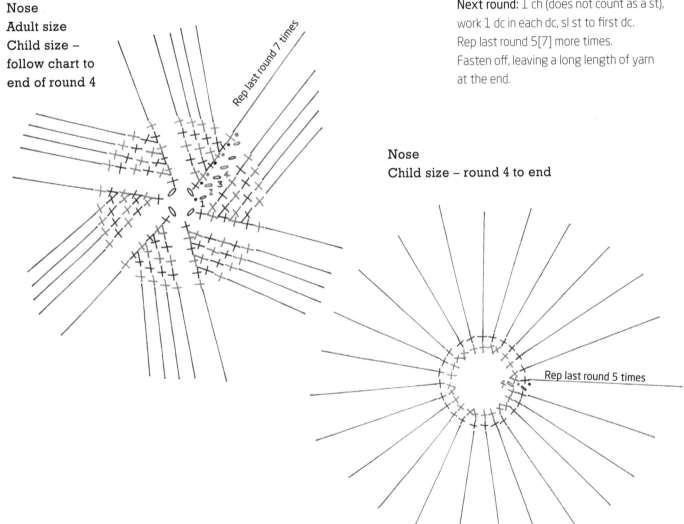

MARKINGS

Tiny (make 5[5])

Starting at the centre of the patch, with 3mm hook and C, make 4 ch and join with a sl st to the first ch to form a ring.

Next: 3 ch (to count as 1 tr), into ring work 2 tr, 2 ch, (3 tr, 2 ch) 4 times into ring, sl st into the third of 3 ch.
Fasten off, leaving a long length of yarn at the end.

Small (make 7[7])

Starting at the centre of the patch, with 3mm hook and C, make 4 ch and join with a sl st to the first ch to form a ring.

Round 1: 3 ch (to count as 1 tr), into ring work 2 tr, 2 ch, (3 tr, 2 ch) 4 times into ring.

Round 2: Work 1 dc into the third of 3 ch to join, work 1 dc into each of the next 2 tr, (2 dc, 2 ch, 2 dc) into next 2 ch sp, *1 dc into next 3 tr, (2 dc, 2 ch, 2 dc) into next 2 ch sp; rep from * 3 more times, sl st into first dc.
Fasten off, leaving a long length of yarn at the end.

Medium (make 7[3])

Starting at the centre of the patch, with 3mm hook and C, make 4 ch and join with a sl st to the first ch to form a ring.

Round 1: 3 ch (to count as 1 tr), into ring work 2 tr, 2 ch, (3 tr, 2 ch) 4 times into ring, sl st into third of 3 ch.

Round 2: 2 ch (to count as first htr), 1 htr into next 2 tr, (2 htr, 2 ch, 2 htr) into next 2 ch sp, *1 htr into next 3 tr, (2 htr, 2 ch, 2 htr) into next 2 ch sp; rep from * 3 more times, sl st into second of 2 ch.
Fasten off, leaving a long length of yarn at the end.

Large (make 0[4])

Starting at the centre of the patch, with 3mm hook and C, make 4 ch and join with a sl st to the first ch to form a ring.

Round 1: Work as for round 1 of medium marking.

Round 2: 3 ch (to count as first tr), 1 tr into next 2 tr, (2 tr, 2 ch, 2 tr) into next 2 ch sp, *1 tr into next 3 tr, (2 tr, 2 ch, 2 tr) into next 2 ch sp; rep from * 3 more times, sl st into third of 3 ch.
Fasten off, leaving a long length of yarn at the end.

Small

Medium

Tiny

Large

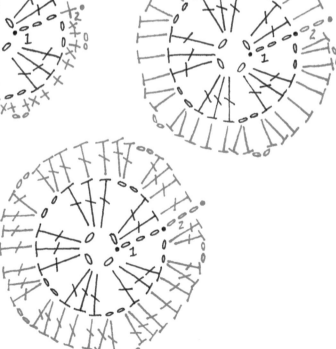

MAKING UP
Edging
With right side of work facing, using 5mm hook and A, rejoin yarn to the back of the hat by the second earflap and follow the edging pattern as for the leopard hat on page 23.

Nose
Stuff the nose lightly to pad it out, keeping a flattened shape. Sew the 12[15] stitches from each side of the opening together to form a straight edge. Stitch the nose in place on the front of the hat with the straight edge sitting just above the second row of edging stitches. Using yarn C and a blunt-ended darning needle, embroider the nostrils by working two straight stitches (see page 155) for each.

Ossicones and ears
Stuff the ossicones firmly and attach them to the top of the hat, stitching all around the lower edge. Push a thin layer of stuffing into the ears, keeping the shape flat. Using the long length of yarn left after fastening off the ear, sew together the 9[12] stitches from each side of the opening to join, forming a straight edge. Turn 1⅜in (3.5cm) over on one corner of the first ear and stitch it down along the straight edge. Repeat with the other ear, folding it at the opposite corner so they mirror each other. Sew the ears in place with the folded edge at the top.

Finishing touches
If making a crocheted lining, attach the twisted cords to the hat after inserting the lining. Place the small black buttons over the larger brown buttons and sew in place for the eyes. Arrange the markings on the front and back of the hat and sew them in place on the main section using the long lengths of yarn left after fastening off. Weave in all the yarn ends. Make two twisted cords (see page 154) using A, each measuring 8[12] in (20[30]cm)] long, using 6[8] strands of yarn. Make two tassels (see page 155) measuring 4[5⅛]in (10[13]cm) long in B, and attach each to one end of the twisted cord, then stitch the other end of the cord to the tip of the earflap.

LINING
See pages 142–5 for how to make and attach a cosy fleece or crocheted lining.

owl

Wide eyes are the stand-out feature of the owl hat.
Tweed yarns echoing the natural hues of the landscape
create additional detail and interest, providing colour
and texture for this wise bird.

MATERIALS

Sirdar Click Chunky, 70% acrylic, 30% wool
    (81yd/75m per 50g ball)
3[3] x 50g balls in 196 Heath (A)
2[2] x 50g balls in 193 Hustler Brown (B)
1[1] x 50g ball in 142 Lamb (C)
5mm (UK6:USH/8) and 6mm (UK4:USJ/10)
    crochet hooks
2 x orange or yellow 1in (2.5cm) diameter buttons
2 x black ⅝in (1.5cm) diameter buttons
Darning needle
Sewing needle
Black thread
Small amount of toy stuffing
Thin card to make tassels

SIZES

To fit: child, up to 20in (51cm) head circumference
[adult, up to 22in (56cm) head circumference]

TENSION

13 sts and 14 rows to 4in (10cm) over double
crochet on 6mm hook. Use larger or smaller hook
if necessary to obtain correct tension.

METHOD

The main part of the hat is crocheted in rounds with the earflaps and facings in rows of double crochet. The wings, eyes and beak use a smaller hook. The wings are crocheted in crocodile stitch, which forms the feather-like pattern for the wings. The eyes are worked in rounds of double crochet, half treble and treble stitches. The shaping around the eyes is created by working first into the front loops of the stitches. A second row is crocheted and then the third is joined to the back loops of the first row of stitches, forming a ridge. The beak is worked in rounds of double crochet and is folded in half and stuffed. Tassels are added to the top of the hat, as well as at the end of the twisted cords.

MAIN PIECE
Both sizes

Starting at the top of the hat, with 6mm hook and A, follow the pattern for the leopard hat main piece on page 14.

EARFLAP FACINGS (MAKE 2)

Omit if you plan to add a crocheted lining.
Both sizes

With 6mm hook and A, follow the earflap facing pattern as for the leopard hat on page 18.
Edging

With 5mm hook and A, follow edging pattern for the earflap facing on page 18.

WINGS (MAKE 2)

Starting at the tip of the wing, with 5mm hook and B, make 9 ch.

Row 1: Work 1 tr into third ch from hook (counts as first 2 tr), (2 ch, miss 2 ch, 2 tr into next ch) twice (3 sets of 2 tr).

Row 2: 1 ch (does not count as a st), miss the first set of 2 tr, work 5 tr down the post of the first of the next 2 tr by taking the hook behind the stitch then back around to the front of the work, rather than into the top of the stitch as usual (see illustration), make 1 ch, work 5 tr up the post of the second of 2 tr, miss next set of 2 tr, sl st between last set of 2 tr (1 feather).

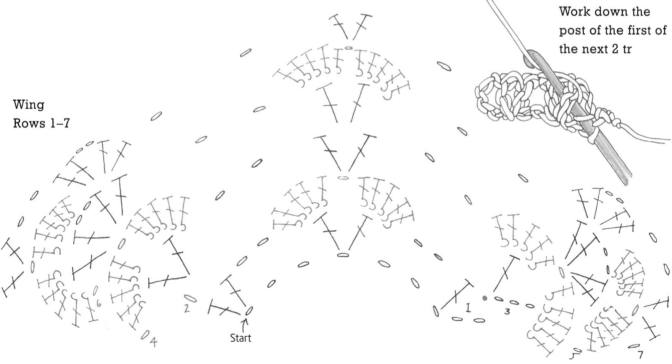

Wing
Rows 1–7

Start

Wing row 2
Work down the post of the first of the next 2 tr

Row 3: 3 ch (counts as first tr), 1 tr between the 2 tr missed on previous row, 2 ch, 2 tr into space in the centre of the feather, 2 ch, 2 tr between the 2 tr missed on previous row (3 sets of 2 tr).

Row 4: 1 ch (does not count as a st), work 5 tr down the post of the first of 2 tr, 1 ch, work 5 tr up the post of the second of 2 tr, miss next set of 2 tr; work 5 tr down the post of the first of the next 2 tr, 1 ch, work 5 tr up the post of the second of 2 tr (2 feathers).

Row 5: 1 ch (does not count as a st), (2tr, 2ch, 2tr) into space in centre of first feather, 2 ch, 2 tr between the 2 tr missed on previous row, 2ch, (2tr, 2ch, 2tr) into space in centre of next feather (5 sets of 2 tr).

Row 6: 1 ch (does not count as a st), work 5 tr down the post of the first of 2 tr, 1 ch, work 5 tr up the post of the second of 2 tr, (miss next set of 2 tr, work 5 tr down the post of the first of the next set of 2 tr, 1 ch, work 5 tr up the post of the second of 2 tr) twice (3 feathers).

Row 7: 1 ch (does not count as a st), 2 tr into space in centre of first feather, *2 ch, (2tr, 2ch, 2tr) between the 2 tr missed on previous row, 2 ch, 2 tr into space in centre of next feather, rep from * once (7 sets of 2 tr).

Row 8: 1 ch (does not count as a st), work 5 tr down the post of the first of the 2 tr, 1 ch, work 5 tr up the post of the second of 2 tr, (miss next set of 2 tr, work 5 tr down the post of the first of the next set of 2 tr, 1 ch, work 5 tr up the post of the second of 2 tr) 3 times (4 feathers).

Row 9: 1 ch (does not count as a st), 2 tr into space in centre of first feather, (2 ch, 2 tr between the 2 tr missed on previous row, 2 ch, 2 tr into space in centre of next feather) 3 times (7 sets of 2 tr).

Row 10: As row 8.

Row 11: As 9.

Row 12: As 8.

Row 13: As 9.

Adult size only

Next: As row 8.

Next: As row 9.

Wing
Rows 7–13[15] and shape top of wing

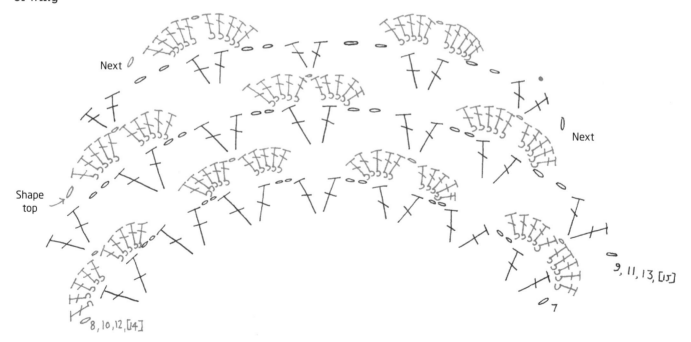

Shape top of wing

Both sizes

Next: 1 ch (does not count as a st), miss the first set of 2 tr, (work 5 tr down the post of the first of the next 2 tr, 1 ch, work 5 tr up the post of the second of 2 tr, miss next set of 2 tr) twice, work 5 tr down the post of the first of the next 2 tr, 1 ch, work 5 tr up the post of the second of 2 tr, sl st between last set of 2 tr (3 feathers).

Next: 1 ch (does not count as a st), 2 tr into space in centre of first feather, (2 ch, 2tr between the 2 tr missed on previous row, 2 ch, 2 tr into space in centre of next feather) twice (5 sets of 2 tr).

Next: 1 ch (does not count as a st), (miss the first set of 2 tr, work 5 tr down the post of the first of the next 2 tr, 1 ch, work 5 tr up the post of the second of 2 tr) twice, sl st between last set of 2 tr (2 feathers).

Fasten off, leaving a long length of yarn at the end.

KEY

⟋ chain (ch)

• slip stitch (sl st)

+ double crochet (dc)

✕✕ dc2inc

T half treble (htr)

Ŧ treble (tr)

⊽ htr2inc

⊻ tr2inc

⌇ treble around post of stitch

∪ work into front loop only

∩ work into back loop only

EYES (MAKE 2)

With 6mm hook and C, make 4 ch and sl st to first ch to form a ring.

Round 1 (RS): 1 ch (does not count as a st), work 6[7] dc into ring, sl st to first dc (6[7] sts).

Round 2 (inc): 3 ch (counts as first tr), work 1 tr into the same st, (tr2inc) 5[6] times, sl st to third of 3 ch (12[14] sts).

Round 3 (inc): 3 ch (counts as first tr), 1 tr into the same st, (tr2inc) 11[13] times, sl st to third of 3 ch (24[28] sts).

Eye

Adult size

Rounds 1–5 and next row

Round 4 (inc): 2 ch (counts as first htr), 1 htr in same st, (1 htr, htr2inc) 11[13] times, 1 htr in next st, sl st to second of 2 ch (36[42] sts).

Eye shaping

Join in yarn A.

Round 5: 1 ch (does not count as a st), work 1 dc in next 10[12] htr, 1 htr in the front loop only of the next 2 htr, work 1 tr in the front loop only of the next 22[26] htr, 1 htr in the front loop only of the next 2 htr, sl st to first dc, turn.

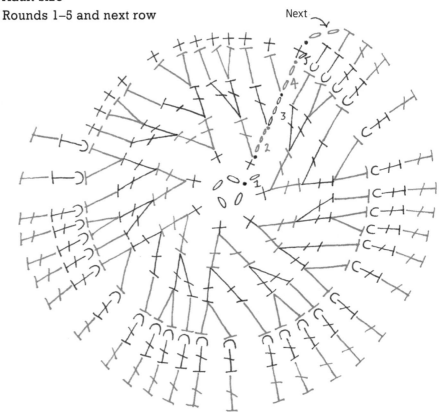

Eye
Child size
Rounds 1–5
and next row

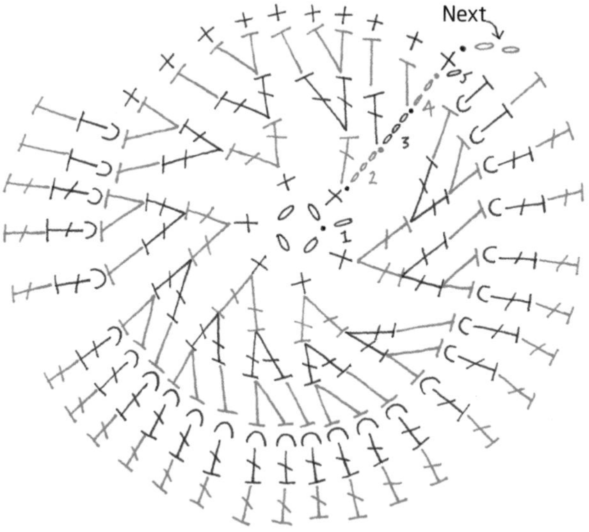

The following is worked in rows:
Next (WS): 2 ch (counts as first htr),
working into both loops of each st, work
1 htr in the next htr, 1 tr in the next
22[26] tr, 1 htr in the next 2 htr, turn.
Create ridge
Next: 1 ch (does not count as a st), fold
the previous row of stitches over the
stitches of round 5, with WS together.
Work 1 dc into each of the next 26[30]
sts of the previous row and the back loops
of the stitches of round 4 at the same
time to join. This will form a lip around the
majority of the edge of the eye.
Fasten off, leaving a long length of yarn
A at the end.

Eye
Create ridge
Adult size

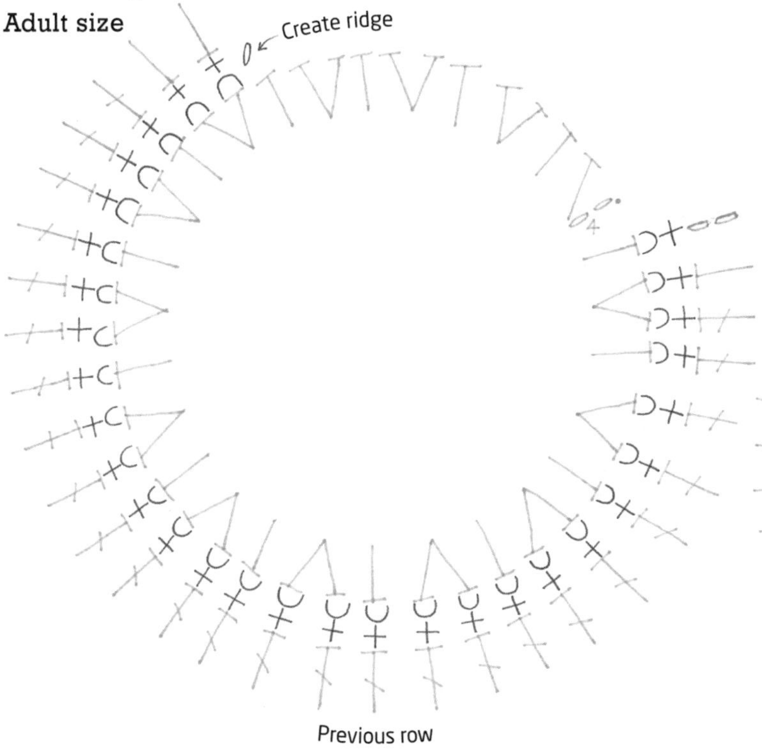

Create ridge

Previous row

Work into each st of the previous row and back
loops only of round 4 at the same time to join

Eye
Create ridge
Child size

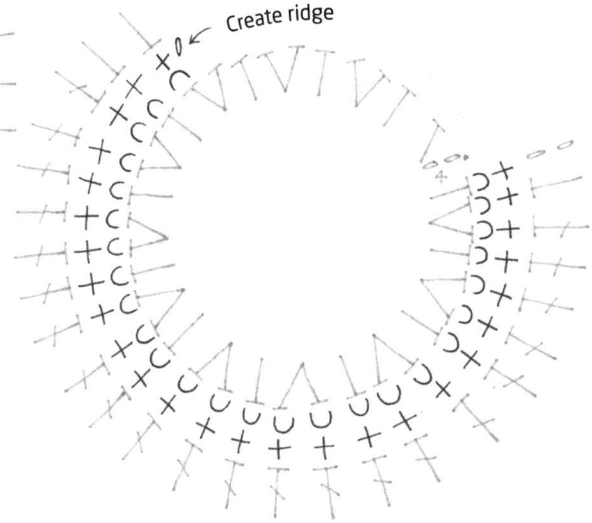

Create ridge

Work into each st of the previous row and back
loops only of round 4 at the same time to join

BEAK

With 5mm hook and B, make 4 ch and join with a sl st to first ch to form a ring.

Round 1: 1 ch (does not count as a st), work 6[7] dc into the ring (6[7] sts).

Round 2 (inc): 1 ch (does not count as a st), (dc2inc) 6[7] times, sl st to the first dc (12[14] sts).

Round 3 (inc): 1 ch (does not count as a st), (dc2inc, 1 dc) 6[7] times, sl st to the first dc (18[21] sts).

Sl st to next st and fasten off, leaving a long length of yarn.

Beak
Child size

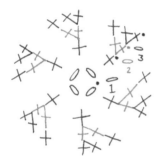

Beak
Adult size

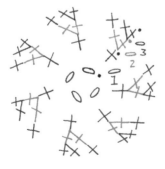

MAKING UP
Edging

With right side of work facing, using 5mm hook and A, rejoin yarn to the back of the hat by the second ear flap and follow the edging pattern as for the leopard hat on page 23.

Eyes

Join the eyes by sewing together a few stitches so the start of the raised lip is in the centre between the eyes and the other end is in line with the lower edge. Position the crocheted eyes just above the edging on the front of the hat and attach with the length of yarn left after fastening off. Sew around the last round of double crochet stitches so that the ridge stands away from the main part of the hat. Stitch the eyes down at the lower edge where there is no ridge. Place the small black buttons over the larger orange or yellow buttons and sew onto the crocheted circles to finish the eyes.

Beak

Fold the crocheted circular piece in half. With the length of yarn left after fastening off, stitch the curved edges together, leaving a small opening. Push a little stuffing through the opening to fill the beak before stitching closed. Sew the beak in place in between the eyes with the curved side facing out, stitching all around it to secure it in position.

Wings

If making a crocheted lining, attach the wings and twisted cords to the earflaps after inserting the lining. Press the wings with a cool iron. Position each wing over the earflaps and sew in place using yarn left after fastening off.

Finishing touches

Weave in all the yarn ends. Make two twisted cords (see page 154) using A, each measuring 8[12]in (20[30]cm) long, using 6[8] strands of yarn. Make two tassels (see page 155) measuring 4[5⅛] in (10[13]cm) long in C, and attach each to one end of the twisted cord, then stitch the other end of the cord to the tip of the earflap. Make two tassels measuring 3[4] in (7.5[10]cm) long in A. Sew to each side of the top of the hat.

LINING

See pages 142–5 for how to make and attach a cosy fleece or crocheted lining.

rabbit

The fleecy yarn creates a lovely furry rabbit, making
this hat really cosy. It is quite difficult to see
the stitches through the 'fur', but holding
it up to a light or window will help.

MATERIALS

Bergère de France Toison, 77% acrylic, 20%
    worsted wool, 3% polyamide (76yd/70m
    per 50g ball)
4[4] x 50g balls in 24540 Castor (A)
1[1] x 50g ball in 25391 Chevalier (B)
1[1] x 50g ball in 22546 Hermine (C)
Oddment of DK yarn in light brown (D)
3mm (UK11:US-), 3.5mm (UK9:USE/4) and 4.5mm
    (UK7:US7) crochet hooks
2 x white ¾[⅞]in (2[2.25]cm) diameter buttons
2 x black ½[⅝]in (1.25[1.5]cm) diameter buttons
Darning needle
Sewing needle
Black thread
Thin card to make pompoms

SIZES

To fit: child, up to 20in (51cm) head circumference
[adult, up to 22in (56cm) head circumference]

TENSION

13 sts and 14 rows to 4in (10cm) over double
crochet on 4.5mm hook. Use larger or smaller hook
if necessary to obtain correct tension.

METHOD

The main piece, cheeks and nose are all worked in rounds of double crochet. The inner and outer parts of the ears are crocheted in rows and stitched together before attaching them to the hat. Twisted cords and fluffy pompoms provide the finishing touches.

MAIN PIECE
Both sizes

Starting at the top of the hat, with 4.5mm hook and A, follow the pattern for the leopard hat main piece on page 14.

Earflap facings (make 2)

Omit if you plan to add a crocheted lining.
Both sizes
With 4.5mm hook and A, follow the earflap facing pattern as for the leopard hat on page 18.

Edging

With 3.5mm hook and B, follow edging pattern for the earflap facing on page 18.

KEY
- ⌒ chain (ch)
- • slip stitch (sl st)
- + double crochet (dc)
- ×× dc2inc

EARS (MAKE 2)
Both sizes

With 4.5mm hook and A, make 2 ch.
Row 1 (RS): Work 3 dc into second ch from hook, turn (3 sts).
Row 2 (inc): 1 ch (does not count as a st), dc2inc, 1 dc, dc2inc, turn (5 sts).
Row 3: 1 ch (does not count as a st), work 1 dc in each dc, turn.
Row 4 (inc): 1 ch (does not count as a st), dc2inc, 1 dc in next 3 dc, dc2inc, turn (7 sts).
Row 5: 1 ch (does not count as a st), work 1 dc in each dc, turn.
Row 6 (inc): 1 ch (does not count as a st), dc2inc, 1 dc in next 5 dc, dc2inc, turn (9 sts).
Row 7: 1 ch (does not count as a st), work 1 dc in each dc, turn.

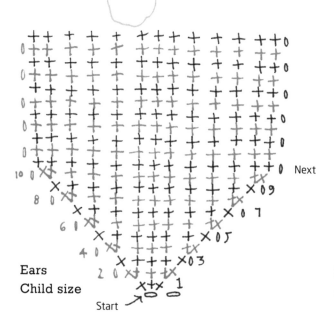

Ears
Child size

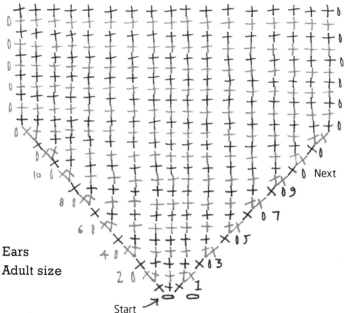

Ears
Adult size

Row 8 (inc): 1 ch (does not count as a st), dc2inc, 1 dc in next 7 dc, dc2inc, turn (11 sts).

Row 9: 1 ch (does not count as a st), work 1 dc in each dc, turn.

Row 10 (inc): 1 ch (does not count as a st), dc2inc, 1 dc in next 9 dc, dc2inc, turn (13 sts).

Adult size only

Next: 1 ch (does not count as a st), work 1 dc in each dc, turn.

Next (inc): 1 ch (does not count as a st), dc2inc, 1 dc in next 11 dc, dc2inc, turn (15 sts).

Next: 1 ch (does not count as a st), work 1 dc in each dc, turn.

Next (inc): 1 ch (does not count as a st), dc2inc, 1 dc in next 13 dc, dc2inc, turn (17 sts).

Both sizes

Next: 1 ch (does not count as a st), work 1 dc in each dc, turn.

Rep last row 10 more times.

Fasten off, leaving a long length of yarn at the end.

INNER EARS (MAKE 2)
Both sizes

With 4.5mm hook and B, make 2 ch.

Row 1 (RS): Work 3 dc into second ch from hook, turn (3 sts).

Row 2 (inc): 1 ch (does not count as a st), dc2inc, 1 dc, dc2inc, turn (5 sts).

Rows 3-4: 1 ch (does not count as a st), work 1 dc in each dc, turn.

Row 5 (inc): 1 ch (does not count as a st), dc2inc, 1 dc in next 3 dc, dc2inc, turn (7 sts).

Rows 6-7: 1 ch (does not count as a st), work 1 dc in each dc, turn.

Row 8 (inc): 1 ch (does not count as a st), dc2inc, 1 dc in next 5 dc, dc2inc, turn (9 sts).

Rows 9-10: 1 ch (does not count as a st), work 1 dc in each dc, turn.

Adult size only

Next (inc): 1 ch (does not count as a st), dc2inc, 1 dc in next 7 dc, dc2inc, turn (11 sts).

Next: 1 ch (does not count as a st), work 1 dc in each dc, turn.

Rep last row once.

Next: 1 ch (does not count as a st), dc2inc, 1 dc in next 9 dc, dc2inc, turn (13 sts).

Both sizes

Next: 1 ch (does not count as a st), work 1 dc in each dc, turn.

Rep last row 10 more times.

Fasten off, leaving a long length of yarn at the end.

**Inner ears
Child size**

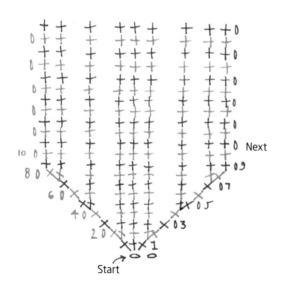

**Inner ears
Adult size**

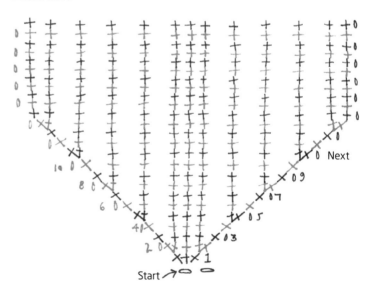

NOSE
Both sizes
With 3mm hook and D, make 4 ch and sl st to first ch to form a ring.

Round 1: 1 ch (does not count as a st), work 6 dc into ring, sl st into first dc (6 sts).

Round 2: 1 ch (does not count as a st), work 1 dc in each dc, sl st to first dc.

Round 3 (inc): 1 ch (does not count as a st), (dc2inc) 6 times, sl st into first dc (12 sts).

Round 4: As round 2.

Adult size only
Next (inc): 1 ch (does not count as a st), (dc2inc, 1 dc) 6 times, sl st into first dc (18 sts).

Next: As round 2.

Both sizes
Sl st to next st and fasten off, leaving a long length of yarn at the end.

CHEEKS (MAKE 2)
Both sizes
With 4.5mm hook and B, make 4 ch and sl st to first ch to form a ring.

Round 1: 1 ch (does not count as a st), work 6 dc into ring, sl st into first dc (6 sts).

Round 2 (inc): 1 ch (does not count as a st), (dc2inc) 6 times, sl st into first dc (12 sts).

Round 3 (inc): 1 ch (does not count as a st), (dc2inc, 1 dc) 6 times, sl st into first dc (18 sts).

Adult size only
Round 4 (inc): 1 ch (does not count as a st), (dc2inc, 2 dc) 6 times, sl st into first dc (24 sts).

Fasten off, leaving a long length of yarn at the end.

Nose
Adult size
Child size – follow chart to end of round 4

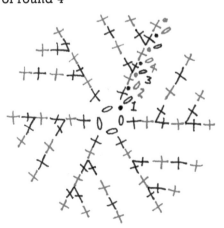

Cheeks
Child size – rounds 1–3
Adult size – rounds 1–4

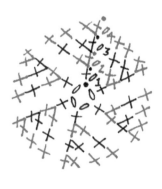

MAKING UP
Edging
With right side of work facing, using 3.5mm hook and B, rejoin yarn to the back of the hat by the second earflap and follow the edging pattern as for the leopard hat on page 23.

Ears
With RS together sew the inner to the outer ear, leaving lower edge open. Turn RS out, positioning the inner ear so it sits centrally with a slight overlap each side of the larger outer piece. Join the lower edges. Bring the two corners of each side from the lower edge of the ear to the middle to shape. Stitch to hold in place. Attach to the main section of the hat.

Cheeks
Sew the cheeks to the face, around ⅝in (1.5cm) from the lower edge, setting them close together.

Nose
Flatten the nose and sew the 6[9] stitches from each side of the top edge together to form a triangular shape. With the stitched edge at the top, sew the nose to centre front of hat, in between the top shaping of the cheeks.

Finishing touches
If making a crocheted lining, attach the twisted cords to the hat after inserting the lining. Weave in all the yarn ends. Make two twisted cords (see page 154) measuring 8[12]in (20[30]cm) long in A, using 6[8] strands of yarn. Make two 2[2⅜]in (5[6]cm) pompoms (see page 155) in C and attach each to one end of the twisted cord, then stitch the other end of the cord to the tip of the earflap. Place the small black buttons over the larger white buttons and sew in place for the eyes.

LINING
See pages 142–5 for how to make and attach a cosy fleece or crocheted lining.

lining your hat

sewing in a
fleece lining

Choose a stretch fabric that feels soft to the touch
to line your animal hat and make it even cosier.

MATERIALS

22in x 22in (56cm x 56cm) [25in x
    25in (63.5cm x 63.5cm)] of stretch
    fabric, such as polar fleece or jersey
Matching thread
Needle
Dressmaking pins
Squared pattern paper
Pencil
Scissors

METHOD

1 Scale the pattern template to size, transferring all the markings onto the paper. Cut out the pattern, following the continuous line. Seam allowances of ⅝in (1.5cm) are included in the pattern. Place the pattern on the folded fleece, ensuring the fold indicated on the pattern is placed exactly on the fold of the fabric. Pin the pattern in position and cut out the fabric.

2 Stitch the darts indicated on the pattern template. Cut to within ½in (1.25cm) of the point of the dart and press open. With right sides together, pin and stitch the main seam, allowing a ⅝in (1.5cm) seam. Trim the seam and cut notches in the curve, taking care not to cut into the stitching.

3 Turn under a hem of ⅝in (1.5cm) and pin to the inside of the hat, just above the crocheted edging or the ribbed pattern, with the main seam of the lining at the centre back of the hat. Ease the fabric evenly around the lower edge. Slip stitch in place by hand. Work a few stitches through the top of the crown into the crocheted hat to keep the lining in place.

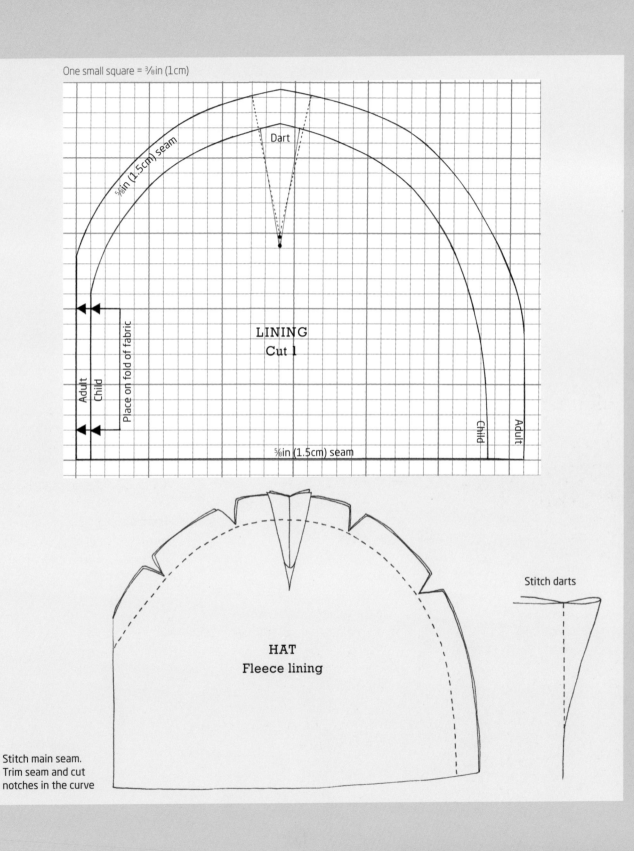

One small square = ³⁄₈in (1cm)

⅝in (1.5cm) seam

Dart

LINING
Cut 1

Place on fold of fabric

Adult
Child

Child
Adult

⅝in (1.5cm) seam

HAT
Fleece lining

Stitch darts

Stitch main seam.
Trim seam and cut
notches in the curve

crocheted lining

Use the same yarn and hook as for the main part of the hat you are making to crochet a cosy lining in a matching or contrasting colour.

MATERIALS

3 ½oz (100g) of the yarn used for the project
Refer to the crochet hooks used for the main part and edging for the sizes you will need for the lining and edging
Darning needle

METHOD

As earflap facings are worked into the crocheted lining, omit them from the main animal hat pattern. Attach the lining after adding the features of the animal and before stitching the twisted cords to the earflaps. If making an owl or parrot hat, sew on the wings after attaching the lining.

For the frog and duck hats

Starting at the top of the hat, with specified hook and yarn, follow the pattern for the leopard hat main piece on page 14 to the end of round 10[11].
Next: 1 ch (does not count as a st), work 1 dc in each dc, sl st into first dc.

Frog hat only

Next: Rep last round 10[13] times more. Fasten off, leaving a long length of yarn. Follow the first 21[24] rounds of the chart for the leopard hat on page 14.

Duck hat only

Next: Rep last round 12[15] times more. Fasten off, leaving a long length of yarn. Follow the first 23[27] rounds of the chart for the leopard hat on page 14.

Making up

With right sides together, matching the centre back, slip the lining inside the hat so the lower edge of it is just above the ribbing. Thread the length of yarn left after fastening off onto a blunt-ended darning needle and sew the lining into the hat, stitching all around the lower edge. Work a few stitches through the top of the hat to hold the lining in place.

FOR ALL HATS WITH EARFLAPS

Starting at the top of the hat, with specified hook and yarn, follow the pattern and charts for the leopard hat main piece and earflaps on pages 14–16. Follow the chart for the leopard hat on page 14[15].

MAKING UP
Edging

With right side of work facing, using the specified hook and yarn used for the edging, rejoin the yarn to the back of the hat by the second earflap and follow the first round of the edging pattern as for the leopard hat on page 23.

Next: With wrong sides together, slip the lining inside the main piece and work 1 ch (does not count as a st).

Working into the stitches of both the main piece and lining at the same time to join, work 1 dc in each of the 10[12] dc across the back of the hat, ***work 1 dc into each of the next 10[12] dc down one side of the earflap, dc2inc, 1 dc into next dc, dc2inc, 1 dc into each of the next 10[12] dc up the other side of the earflap***, work 1 dc into each of the next 24 dc across the front of the hat, rep from *** to *** to finish the edging of the second earflap (84[94] sts).

Sl st to next st and fasten off. Weave in the ends.

basic techniques

getting started

A list of materials required to make each hat can be found at the beginning of each pattern, so you can gather together the right size hooks, enough yarn and any other items that you need before you begin.

SIZING

The finished animal hats are intended to fit children up to 20in (51cm) head circumference, and adults up to 22in (56cm) head circumference.

TENSION

Checking the tension before starting a project is vital, since this will affect the size and look of the finished piece. The tension is the number of rows and stitches per square inch or centimetre of crocheted fabric.

Stitches

Using the same size hook and type of stitch as in the pattern, work a sample of around 5in (12.5cm) and then smooth it out on a flat surface. Place a ruler horizontally across the work and mark 4in (10cm) with pins. Count the number of stitches between the pins, including half stitches. This will give you the tension of the stitches.

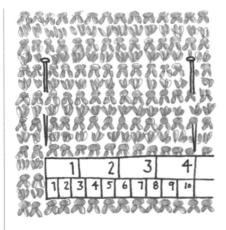

stitches

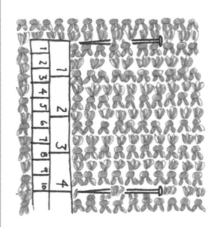

rows

Rows

Measure the tension of the rows by placing a ruler vertically over the work and mark 4in (10cm) with pins. Count the number of rows between the pins.

If the number of stitches and rows is greater than those stated in the pattern, your tension is tighter and you should use a larger hook. If the number of stitches and rows is fewer than those stated in the pattern, your tension is looser, so you should use a smaller hook.

HOOKS

Sizes vary widely, from tiny hooks that produce a very fine stitch when used with threads to oversized hooks for working with several strands of yarn at one time to create a bulky fabric. Using a larger or smaller hook will change the look of the fabric and will also affect the tension and the amount of yarn required.

NEEDLES

A blunt-ended darning or tapestry needle is used to sew the projects together. The rounded end will prevent any snagging and the large eye makes it easy to thread the needle with the thick yarns.

SUBSTITUTING YARNS

When substituting yarns, it is important to calculate the number of balls required by the number of yards or meters per ball rather than the weight of the yarn because this varies according to the fibre. Tension is also important. Always work a tension swatch in the yarn you wish to use before starting a project.

READING PATTERNS

The animal-hat patterns are written for children's and adults' sizes. The children's size is given first and where the adults' instructions differ, the adjustment is given inside the square brackets [ ]. If 0 appears in the instructions, then no stitches or rows are to be worked for this size. Where there is no bracket after the stitches or rows given, the instructions refer to both sizes.

READING CHARTS

Each symbol on a chart represents a stitch; every round or horizontal row represents one round or row of crochet. For rounds of crochet, read the chart counterclockwise, starting at the centre and working out to the last round on the chart.

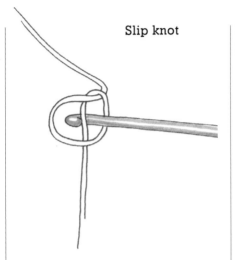

Slip knot

Slip knot

Take the end of the yarn and form it into a ring. Holding it in place between thumb and forefinger, insert the hook through the ring, catch the long end that is attached to the ball, and draw it back through. Keeping the yarn looped on the hook, pull through until the loop closes around the hook, ensuring it is not tight. Pulling on the short end of yarn will loosen the knot; pulling on the long end will tighten it.

Holding the hook

HOLDING THE WORK
Hook

Hold the hook as you would a pencil, bringing your middle finger forwards to rest near the tip of the hook. This will help control the movement of the hook, while the fingers of your other hand will regulate the tension of the yarn. The hook should face you, pointing slightly downwards. The motion of the hook and yarn should be free and even, not tight. This will come with practice.

Yarn

To hold your work and control the tension, pass the yarn over the first two fingers of your left hand (right if you are left-handed), under the third finger and around the little finger, and let the yarn fall loosely to the ball. As you work, take the stitch you made between the thumb and forefinger of the same hand. The hook is usually inserted through the top two loops of a stitch as you work, unless otherwise stated in a pattern. A different effect is produced when only the back loop of the stitch is picked up.

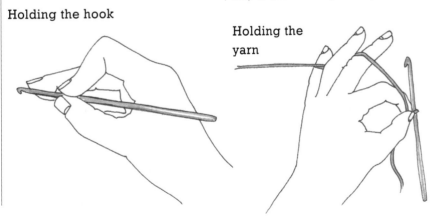

Holding the yarn

crochet stitches

Here is all the basic information you need to crochet
your animal hat. A simple slip knot (see page 149) is the
starting point for the various stitches that you will use.

CHAIN (CH)

1 Pass the hook under and over the yarn
that is held taught between the first
and second fingers. This is called 'yarn
round hook' (yrh). Draw the yarn through
the loop on the hook. This makes one
chain (ch).

2 Repeat step 1, keeping the thumb
and forefinger of the left hand close to
the hook, until you have as many chain
stitches as required.

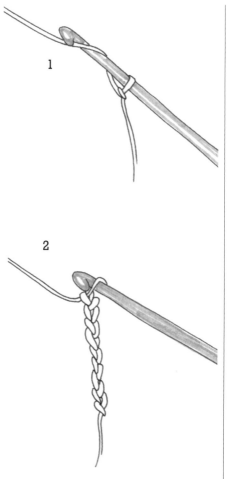

SLIP STITCH (SL ST)

Make a practice chain of 10. Insert hook
into first stitch, yrh, draw through both
loops on hook. This forms 1 sl st. Continue
to the end. This will give you 10 slip
stitches (10 sts).

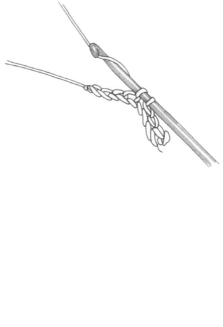

DOUBLE CROCHET (DC)

1 Make a practice chain of 17. Miss the first chain. Insert hook from front into the next stitch, yarn round hook and draw back through the stitch (2 loops on hook).

2 Yarn round hook and draw through 2 loops (1 loop on hook). This makes one double crochet. Repeat steps 1 and 2 to end. On the foundation chain of 17 sts you should have 16 double crochet stitches (16 sts).

Next row
Turn the work so the reverse side faces you. Make 1 chain (ch). This is the turning chain, which helps keep a neat edge and does not count as a stitch. Rep steps 1 and 2 to the end of the row. Continue until the desired number of rows is complete. Fasten off.

FASTENING OFF

When you have finished, fasten off by cutting the yarn around 4¾in (12cm) from the work. Draw the loose end through the remaining loop, pulling it tightly.

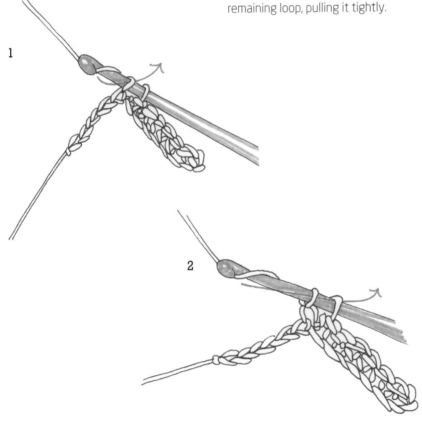

HALF TREBLE (HTR)

1 Make a practice chain of 17. Miss the first 2 chain stitches (these count as the first half treble stitch). Yarn round hook (yrh), insert hook into the next st, yarn round hook and draw back through stitch (3 loops on hook).

2 Yarn round hook, draw through all 3 loops (1 loop on hook). This forms 1 half treble (htr). Repeat steps 1 and 2 to the end of the row. On the foundation chain of 17 sts you should have 16 half trebles (16 sts), including the 2 ch at the beginning of the row, which is counted as the first stitch.

Next row
Turn the work so the reverse side faces you. Make 2 ch to count as the first half treble. Miss the first stitch of the previous row. Repeat steps 1 and 2 for the next 14 htr of the last row, work 1 htr in the second of the 2 ch at the end of the row. Continue until the desired number of rows is complete. Fasten off.

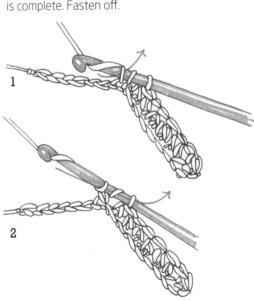

TREBLE (TR)

1 Make a practice chain of 18. Miss the first 3 chain stitches (these count as the first treble stitch). Yarn round hook (yrh), insert hook into the next st, yarn round hook and draw back through stitch (3 loops on hook).

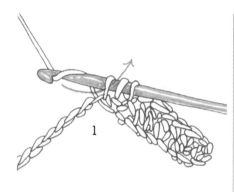

2 Yarn round hook, draw through 2 loops (2 loops on hook).

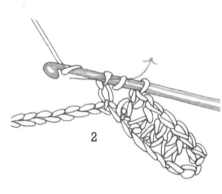

3 Yarn round hook, draw through 2 loops (1 loop on hook). This forms 1 treble (tr). Repeat steps 1–3 to end of row. On the foundation chain of 18 sts you should have 16 trebles (16 sts), including the 3 ch at the beginning of the row, counted as the first stitch.

Next row

Turn the work so the reverse side faces you. Make 3 ch to count as the first treble. Miss the first stitch of the previous row. Repeat steps 1–3 to the end of the row, working 1 tr into the third of the 3 ch at the beginning of the last row. Continue until the desired number of rows is complete. Fasten off.

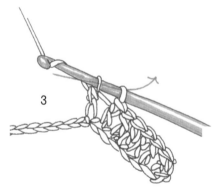

INCREASING

To increase one double crochet (dc2inc), half treble (htr2inc) or treble stitch (tr2inc), work two stitches into one stitch of the previous row.

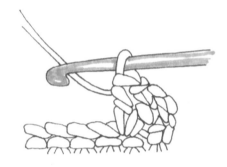

DECREASING

To decrease one double crochet (dc2dec), insert the hook into the next stitch, yarn round hook and draw back through the stitch (2 loops on hook); insert the hook into the following stitch, yarn round hook and draw back through the stitch (3 loops on hook), yarn round hook and draw through all three loops on the hook.

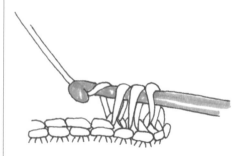

JOINING IN COLOURS

At the beginning of a round or row

When joining in a new colour at the beginning of a round or row, catch the yarn in the new colour and draw through the stitch. Work the first stitch in the new colour into the same place as the join.

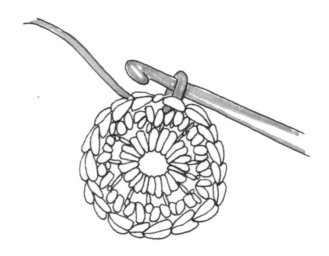

In the middle of a row

1 When joining in a new colour in the middle of a row, it is worked into the stitch preceding the one that the new shade is to start. To join in the new colour, insert hook in next stitch, yarn round hook in the first colour, draw back through the stitch (2 loops on hook), yarn round hook with the new colour, draw through both loops on hook. Continue in the new colour.

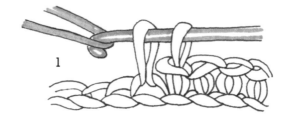

2 The colour that is not in use can be carried across the back of the work and hidden along the line of stitches being made using the contrast colour, keeping the crocheted fabric neat so either side of the finished work can be used. This method is used at the beginning of the face shaping for the husky hat on page 96.

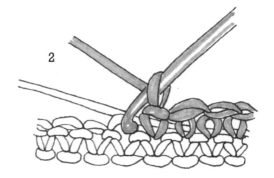

Alternatively, several small balls of yarn can be wound beforehand to use separately for each block of colour, as in the tiger hat on page 85.

finishing touches

The added crocheted features and buttons give character to the hats. Twisted cords tipped with pompoms or tassels decorate the ends of the earflaps as well as holding them down so they keep your ears warm.

TWISTED CORD

1 Measure 6[8] strands of around ⅞[1⅓]yd (0.8[1.2]m) lengths of yarn. This will give you extra length to sew and weave the ends into the earflaps. Knot the ends of the yarn together. Slip one end over a coat hook and insert a pencil into the other end. Hold the pencil between the thumb and forefinger, keeping the yarn taut. Turn the pencil clockwise to twist the strands.

2 Continue turning the pencil until the strands are tightly twisted. Fold them, allowing the two halves to twist together naturally. Remove the pencil and carefully undo the knots. With a strand threaded onto a needle, wind the yarn around the cord near the top and secure with a few stitches. Alternatively, the end can be knotted but it will be bulkier.

STRIPED CORD

1 Measure 3[4] strands of around ⅞[1⅓]yd (0.8[1.2]m) lengths of yarn in each colour. This will give you extra length to sew and weave the ends into the hat earflaps. Fold the lengths of one colour in half and knot the ends together to form a loop of stranded yarn. Thread the 3[4] strands of the remaining colour through the loop and knot those ends together. Slip the knotted end of one loop over a coat hook and insert a pencil through the other loop. Hold the pencil between the thumb and forefinger, keeping the yarn taut. The point where the yarn is intertwined should be in the middle.

2 Turn the pencil clockwise until the strands are tightly twisted. Fold them in the middle, where the two colours meet, and allow them to twist together naturally, producing a striped effect. Finish as for the twisted cord.

POMPOMS

1 Cut two circles of card to the required measurement for each pompom. Make a hole in the centre of each circle. The hole should be around a third of the size of the finished pompom. Thread a blunt needle with a long length of doubled yarn and, with the two circles of card together, wind the yarn through the hole and around the outer edge of the circle. Continue in this way, using new lengths of yarn, until the hole is filled and the circle is covered.

2 Cut through the yarn around the outer edge between the two circles of card. Tie a length of yarn securely around the middle, leaving long ends to attach the pompoms to the twisted cords. Remove the card and trim the pompom, fluffing it into shape.

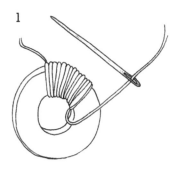

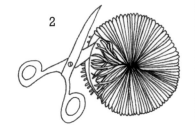

TASSELS

1 Cut a piece of card to the required length of the finished tassel. Wind the yarn around the card to the desired thickness. Break yarn, leaving a long length, and thread it through a needle. Slip the needle through all the loops on the card and tie the yarn tightly at the top edge.

2 Remove the card and wind the yarn around the loops, a little way down from the tied top end, securing with a few stitches and drawing the needle through to the top to leave an end to stitch to the cord. Cut through the folded lower edge and trim to neaten the ends.

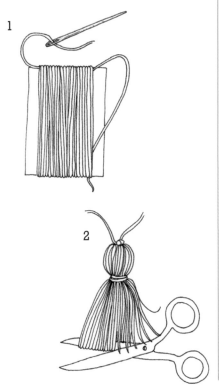

EMBROIDERY STITCHES

These simple stitches are used to add features to the sheep, zebra and giraffe hats on pages 48, 68 and 114.

Fly stitch

1 Bring the yarn through to the front of the work on the left side of the centre of the stitch and hold it down with your left thumb. Insert the needle to the right, in line with the point where it first emerged. Bring the needle back through to the front of the work and a little way down, in line with the centre of the stitch, keeping the yarn under the needle.

2 Insert the needle back into the work to form a V shape with the stitch. Insert the needle lower down, forming a straight line below the V-shaped stitch.

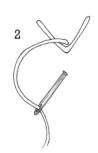

Straight stitch

This is a single stitch that can be worked in varying lengths. It is useful for embroidering short lines.

ABBREVIATIONS

ch	chain
ch sp	chain space
cm	centimetres
dc	double crochet
dc2dec	work 2 double crochet stitches together to decrease
dc2inc	work 2 double crochet stitches into the next stitch to increase
dec	decrease
htr	half treble
htr2inc	work 2 half treble crochet stitches into the next stitch to increase
in	inches
inc	increase
mb	make bobble
rep	repeat
RS	right side
sl st	slip stitch
st(s)	stitch(es)
tr	treble
tr2inc	work 2 treble stitches into the next st to increase
yd	yards
yrh	yarn round hook
WS	wrong side

CONVERSIONS

Steel crochet hook conversions

Metric (mm)	UK	US
0.60	6	14
-	5½	13
0.75	5	12
-	4½	11
1.00	4	10
-	3½	9
1.25	3	8
1.50	2½	7
1.75	2	6
-	1½	5

Aluminium crochet hook conversion

Metric (mm)	UK	US
2.00	14	-
2.25	13	B/1
2.50	12	-
2.75	-	C/2
3.00	11	-
3.25	10	D/3
3.50	9	E/4
3.75	-	F/5
4.00	8	G/6
4.50	7	7
5.00	6	H/8
5.50	5	I/9
6.00	4	J/10
6.50	3	K/10½
7.00	2	-
8.00	0	L/11
9.00	00	M/13
10.00	000	N/15
11.50	-	P/16

UK and US crochet terms

UK crochet terms	US crochet terms
Double crochet	Single crochet
Half treble	Half double crochet
Treble	Double crochet

SUPPLIERS

YARNS

France
Bergère de France
55020 Bar-le-duc Cedex
France
Tel: +33 (0)3 29 79 36 66
www.bergeredefrance.co.uk
www.bergeredefrance.fr

Spain
Katia Yarns
Fil Katia, S. A.
Av Catalunya
s / n – 08296 Castellbell i el Vilar
Barcelona
Tel: +34 93 828 38 19
www.katia.com

UK
Deramores
Units 5–9 Tomas Seth Business Park
Argent Road
Queenborough
ME11 5TS
Tel: +44 (0)8455 194573
www.deramores.com

King Cole Ltd
Merrie Mills
Elliott Street
Silsden
West Yorkshire
BD20 0DE
Tel: +44 (0)1535 650230
www.kingcole.co.uk

Love Knitting Ltd
1–4 Priestley Road
Wardley Industrial Estate
Worsley
Manchester
M28 2LY
Tel: 0845 5760 007
www.loveknitting.com

Sirdar Spinning Ltd
Flanshaw Lane
Wakefield
West Yorkshire
WF2 9ND
Tel: +44 (0)1924 371501
www.sirdar.co.uk

The Stitchery
12–16 Riverside
High Street
Lewes
East Sussex BN7 2RE
Tel: +44 (0)1273 473577
www.the-stitchery.co.uk

USA
Lion Brand
Tel: +1 800 661 7551
www.lionbrand.com

HOOKS

UK
Coats Crafts UK
Green Lane Mill
Holmfirth
West Yorkshire
HD9 2DX
Tel: +44 (0)1484 681 881
www.coatscrafts.co.uk

USA
Purl Soho
459 Broome Street
New York, NY 10013
Tel: +1 212 420 8796
www.purlsoho.com

HABERDASHERY

UK
MacCulloch and Wallis
25–26 Dering Street
London W1S 1AT
Tel: +44 (0)20 7629 0311
Email: info@macculloch.com
www.macculloch-wallis.co.uk

Merchant & Mills Limited
14A Tower Street
Rye
East Sussex
TN31 7AT
Tel: +44 (0)1797 227789
www.merchantandmills.com

Ray Stitch
99 Essex Road
London
N1 2SJ
Tel: +44 (0)20 7704 1060
www.raystitch.co.uk

USA
Brooklyn General Store
128 Union St
Brooklyn
NY 11231
Tel: +1 718 237 7753
www.brooklyngeneral.com

WADDING AND STUFFING

UK
World of Wool
Unit 8 The Old Railway Goods Yard
Scar Lane
Milnsbridge
Huddersfield
West Yorkshire
HD3 4PE
Tel: +44 (0)1484 846 878
www.worldofwool.co.uk

USA
Fabric and Art
101 Boatyard Drive Fort Bragg
California 95437
Tel: +1 707 964 6365
www.fabricandart.com

ABOUT THE AUTHOR

Vanessa Mooncie is a contemporary crochet jewellery designer and maker, silkscreen artist and illustrator. She spent many happy hours as a child learning to crochet and knit with her mother and grandmother. She went on to study fashion and textile design, then became a children's wear designer, illustrator and commercial interior designer. She lives with her family in the English countryside.

AUTHOR'S ACKNOWLEDGMENTS

I would like to thank Wendy McAngus and all at GMC. Thank you very much to Jonathan Bailey for giving me the opportunity to write *Crocheted Animal Hats*. For their continuous support and encouragement, I thank my husband Damian, my children Miriam, Dilys, Flynn and Honey, and my granddaughter Dolly, who have all very kindly and patiently modelled the hats for me as I made them.

PUBLISHER'S ACKNOWLEDGMENTS

GMC would like to thank the following people for their help in creating this book: Chris Gloag for photography, Tiffany from Zone Models, Jen Dodson for hair and make-up, Amelia Holmwood for styling, and Anthony Bailey for still-life shots.

INDEX

To order a book, or to request a catalogue, contact:
GMC Publications, Castle Place, 166 High Street, Lewes, East Sussex, BN7 1XU, United Kingdom
Tel: +44 (0)1273 488005
www.gmcbooks.com